趣味識字
Fun with Chinese
A Chinese Character Learning Curriculum

第三冊

Workbook 3

自序

我是一位在美國的自學媽媽，孩子的中文學習完全由我親自教導。

在傳統教學方式的薰陶下許多家長認為孩子學中文必須先從注音開始，往往也認為中文字筆畫眾多複雜對小孩來說太難。其實對幼兒來說每一個中文字都只是一個圖案，幼兒的記憶力非常強，認字對他們來說並不困難。

我自己的兩個孩子都是從認字開始學習中文的。當初我會設計趣味識字是因為在市面上並沒有找到令我完全滿意的教材，絕大多數的教材都是從注音符號或是筆畫簡單的字開始教學。雖然筆劃較少容易書寫但往往這些字在日常生活上並不常見，在孩子的世界裡更是沒有應用的機會。而市面上認字的教材卻普遍地缺乏動手的參與感。孩子在學習的過程中常常覺得教材枯燥乏味，既沒趣味又缺乏實用性。這樣的學習對孩子來說不但痛苦也沒有效率。使用這些教材後我發現自己一直在動手製作輔助教材來提昇孩子的學習興趣。

我一直深信一定要讓孩子覺得有趣和實用，他們才會有學習的動力，有了動力才會學得好。所以趣味識字的設計是以先教常用字的方式讓孩子能夠快速進入閱讀，因而發覺識字的實用性。當孩子懂得如何應用文字後，學習自信自然就提高了。製作輔助教材時為了幫助孩子加強對生字的記憶，除了使用字卡和遊戲的方式複習，我也設計了一系列的遊戲習題，而這些習題就是趣味識字誕生的前奏。

最後非常感謝您選擇趣味識字做為孩子的教材，也希望這套教材可以幫助您的孩子快樂學習中文。

Preface

I am a homeschooling mom in America who successfully taught my two children to read Chinese at a young age.

Many people think that learning Chinese must start with pinyin because Chinese characters are too complicated and believed to be too difficult for children. However, in children's minds, each Chinese character is just like a picture and memorization is not difficult for them.

Both my children learned to read Chinese beginning with character recognition, yet the process was not easy for me. Existing textbooks often start teaching with pinyin or start with rarely used characters with minimal strokes for writing. Books that emphasize character recognition also tend to be less interactive and less hands-on causing the learning process to be tedious and unmotivating for children. I found myself constantly needing to create my own teaching materials while using these textbooks; and this is the reason for the creation of Fun with Chinese.

Fun with Chinese is designed to teach the most commonly used Chinese characters first, quickly allowing children to be able to read meaningful phrases and sentences from the very beginning. Pictures and games are also used to help with character retention, and each lesson includes reading passages to review previously learned characters.

Today, I am sharing with you this wonderful system that I have used with my own children and hoping to make your child's Chinese learning an easy and enjoyable journey.

— Anchia Tai

關於英文翻譯

習題本中的句子都有中英雙語,希望讓中文不是很好的家長們也有辦法使用教材。其中朗讀句子練習中的英文翻譯也盡量讓句型和中文相對應幫助英文為母語的家長容易理解。

About the English Translations

The English translations in the workbooks are specifically designed in a way to closely match up with the Chinese sentence grammar structure. While this might make the translations grammatically incorrect in English, the design will help English speakers to learn and understand the Chinese sentences better.

關於筆順

本書中的國字筆順是依據中華民國教育部「常用國字標準字體筆順學習網」的筆劃順序彙編。中華民國教育部對於部分筆順有做調整,可能於傳統書寫筆順有所差異,不同華人地區的筆順也可能有所不同。如果本書中的筆順與家長所學的筆順有所差異,請自行調整教學。

About the Stroke Orders

The stroke orders of the characters in this workbook follow the stroke orders provided on the "Learning Program for Stroke Order of Frequently Used Chinese Characters" website of the Ministry of Education, R.O.C. (Taiwan). The authors are aware that there were changes to the stroke orders made by the Ministry of Education as well as regional differences in character stroke orders. Please feel free to make adjustments in teaching if the stroke orders are different in your region.

每當完成一課後請回到本頁將該課的星星塗上顏色。
Please color a star after you have completed a lesson.

四 五 地 出
天
會 藍 他 明
走
飛 子 只
快 紅
日 給 色
跳 兔
學 生 看
氣 就

第一課

Lesson 1 Sì – four

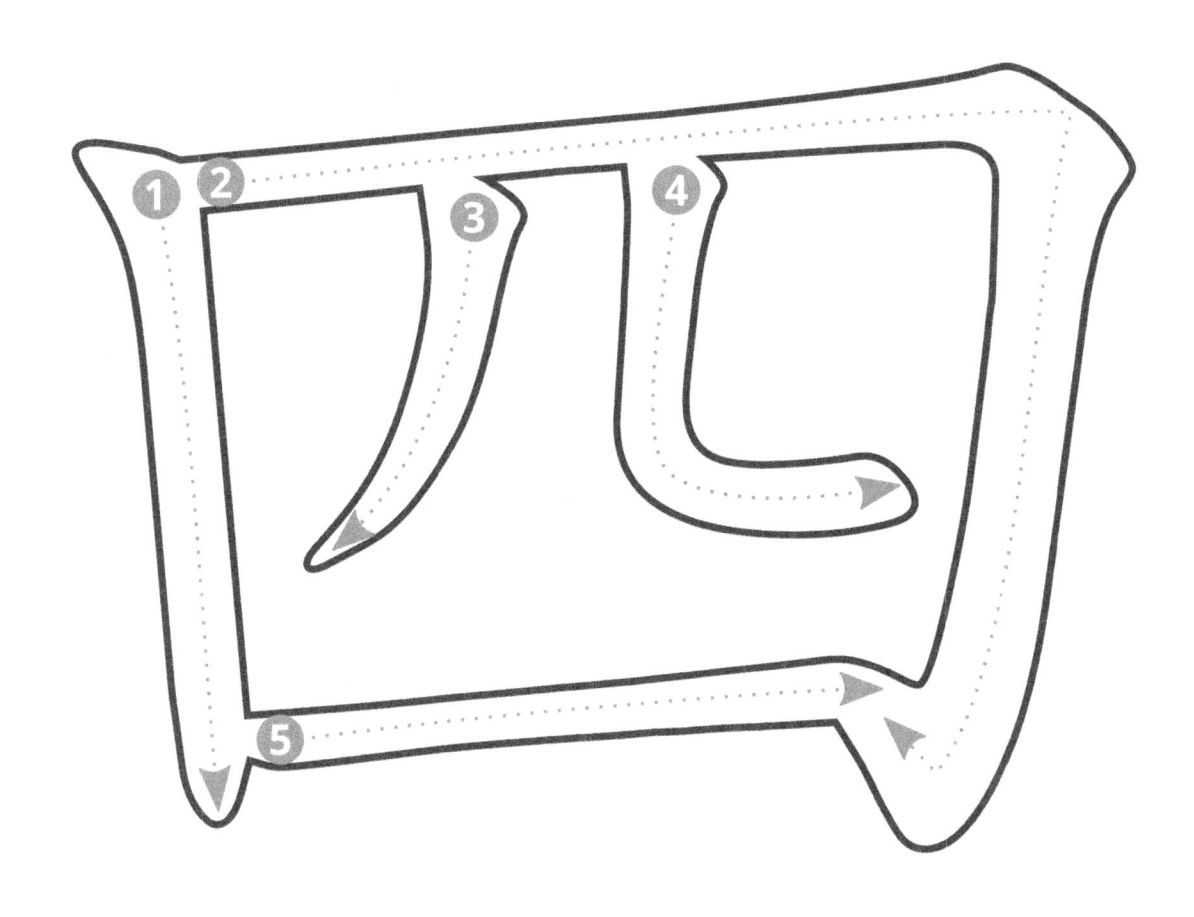

本書中的國字筆順是依據中華民國教育部「常用國字標準字體筆順學習網」的筆劃順序彙編。
The stroke orders of the characters in this workbook follow the stroke orders provided on the "Learning Program for Stroke Order of Frequently Used Chinese Characters" website of the Ministry of Education, R.O.C. (Taiwan).

請將四顆糖果上色。
Please color four candies.

四

4

在圖案旁貼上正確的數量。

Paste the correct quantities into the boxes next to the pictures.

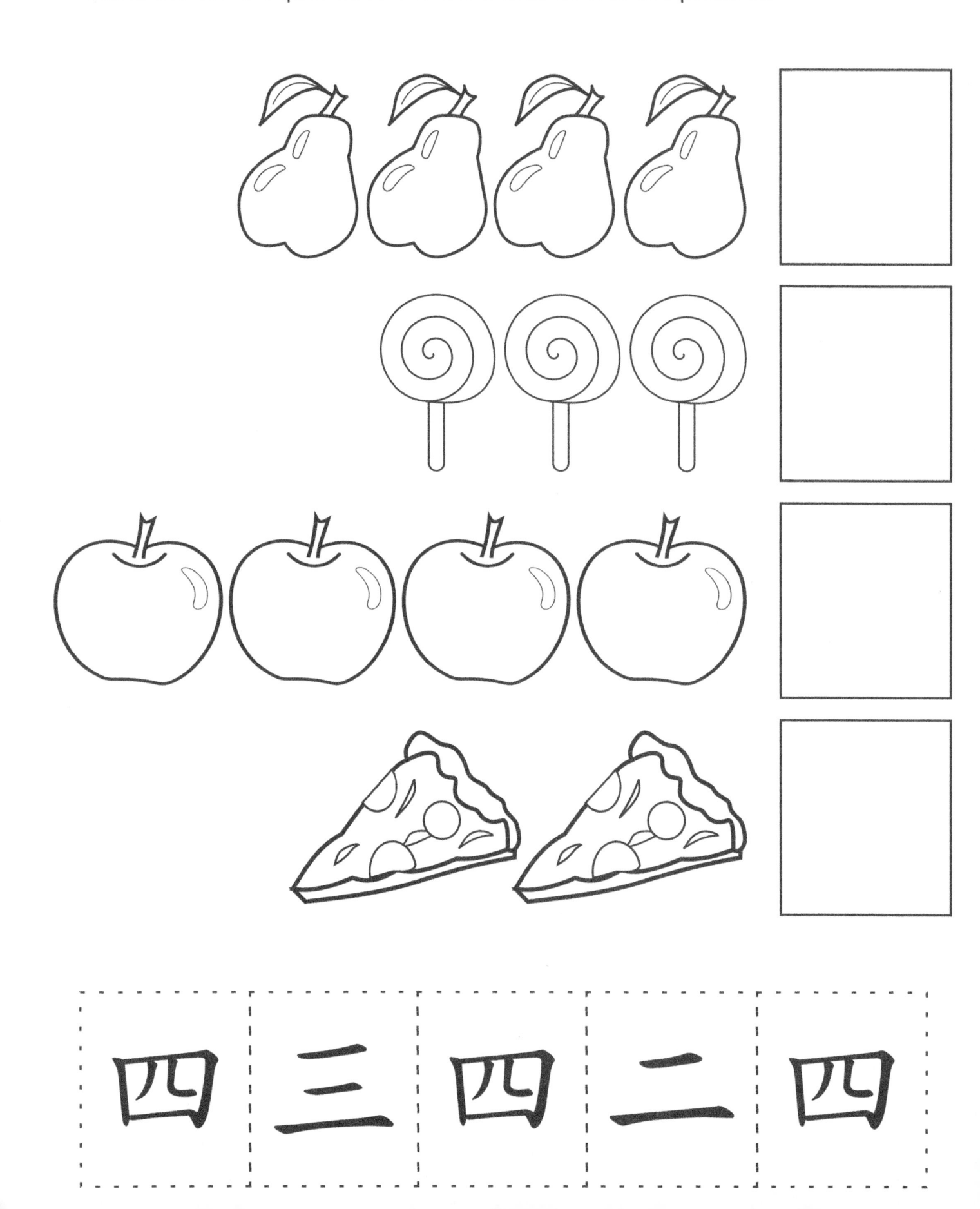

四 三 四 二 四

唸唸看
Read-Aloud

- 四隻小鳥在上頭。
  Four little birds are up there.

- 大貓在家中。
  The big cat is at home.

- 四隻小鳥為什麼不下來玩？
  Why are the four little birds not coming down to play?

- 媽媽說：「小鳥以為貓在下頭。」
  Mom says, "The little birds think the cat is down there."

恭喜你完成了這一課，請回到第一頁將本課的星星塗上顏色。
Congratulations! You have completed a lesson. Please color the star for this lesson on page 1.

第二課

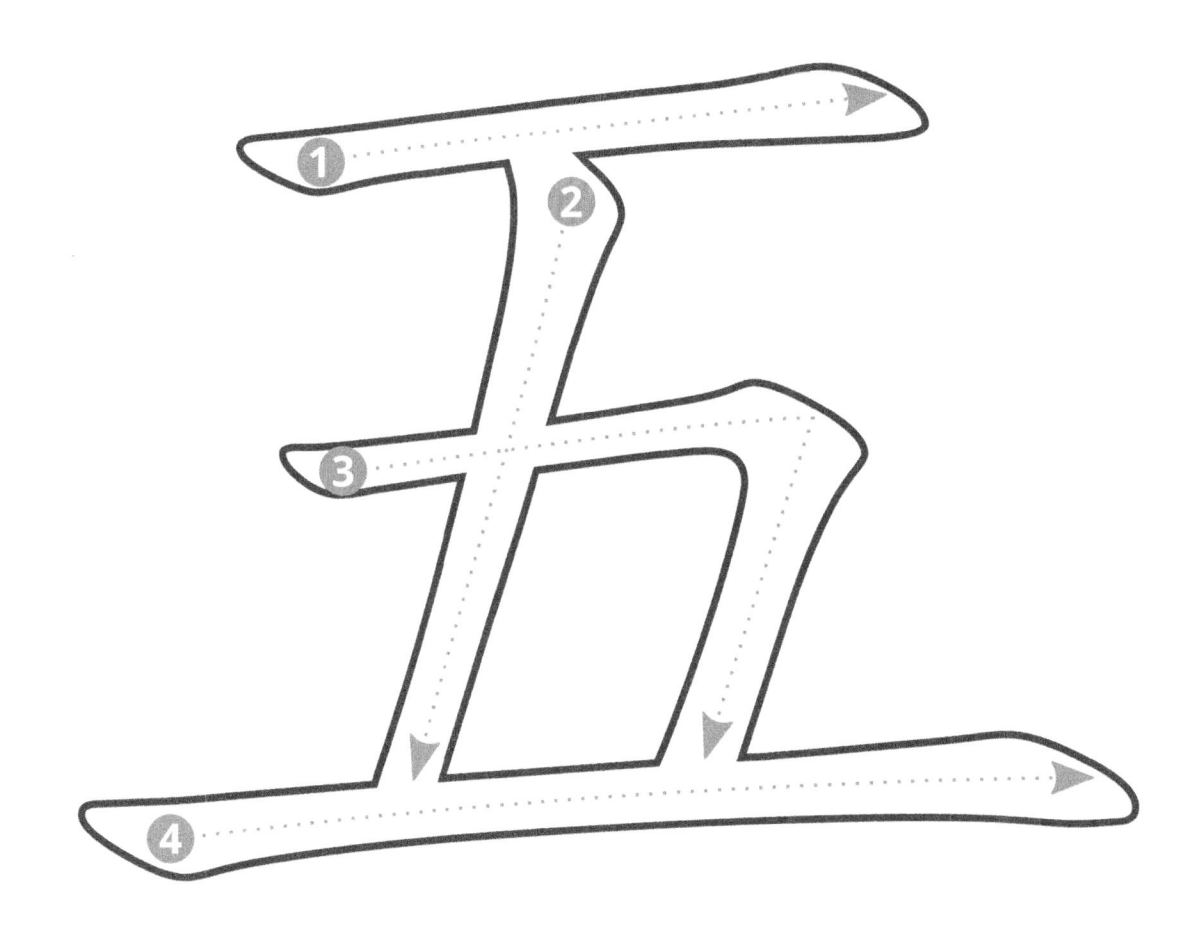

Lesson 2 Wǔ – five

本書中的國字筆順是依據中華民國教育部「常用國字標準字體筆順學習網」的筆劃順序彙編。
The stroke orders of the characters in this workbook follow the stroke orders provided on the "Learning Program for Stroke Order of Frequently Used Chinese Characters" website of the Ministry of Education, R.O.C. (Taiwan).

請依照數字順序連出圖案。
Connect the dots in order to form a picture.

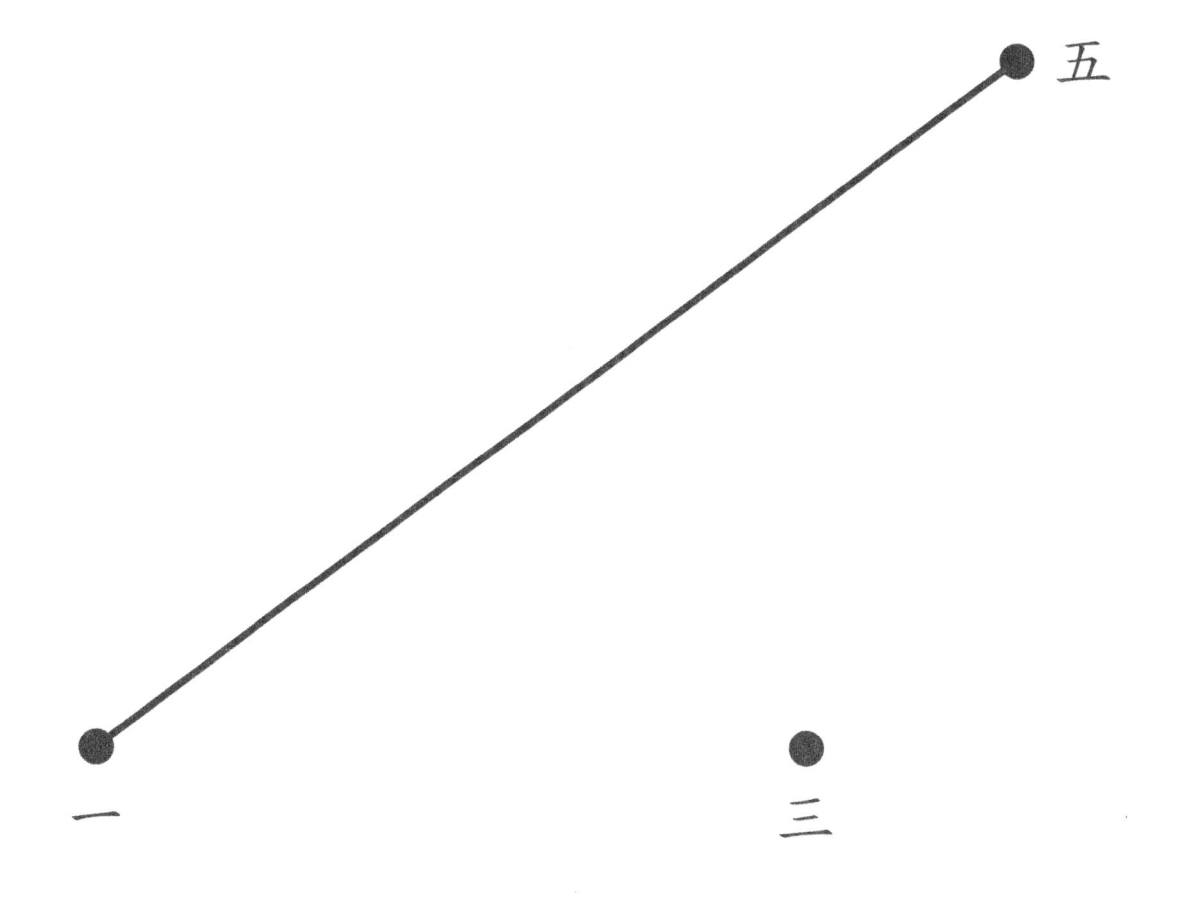

請圈出正確的數量。
Please circle the correct quantities.

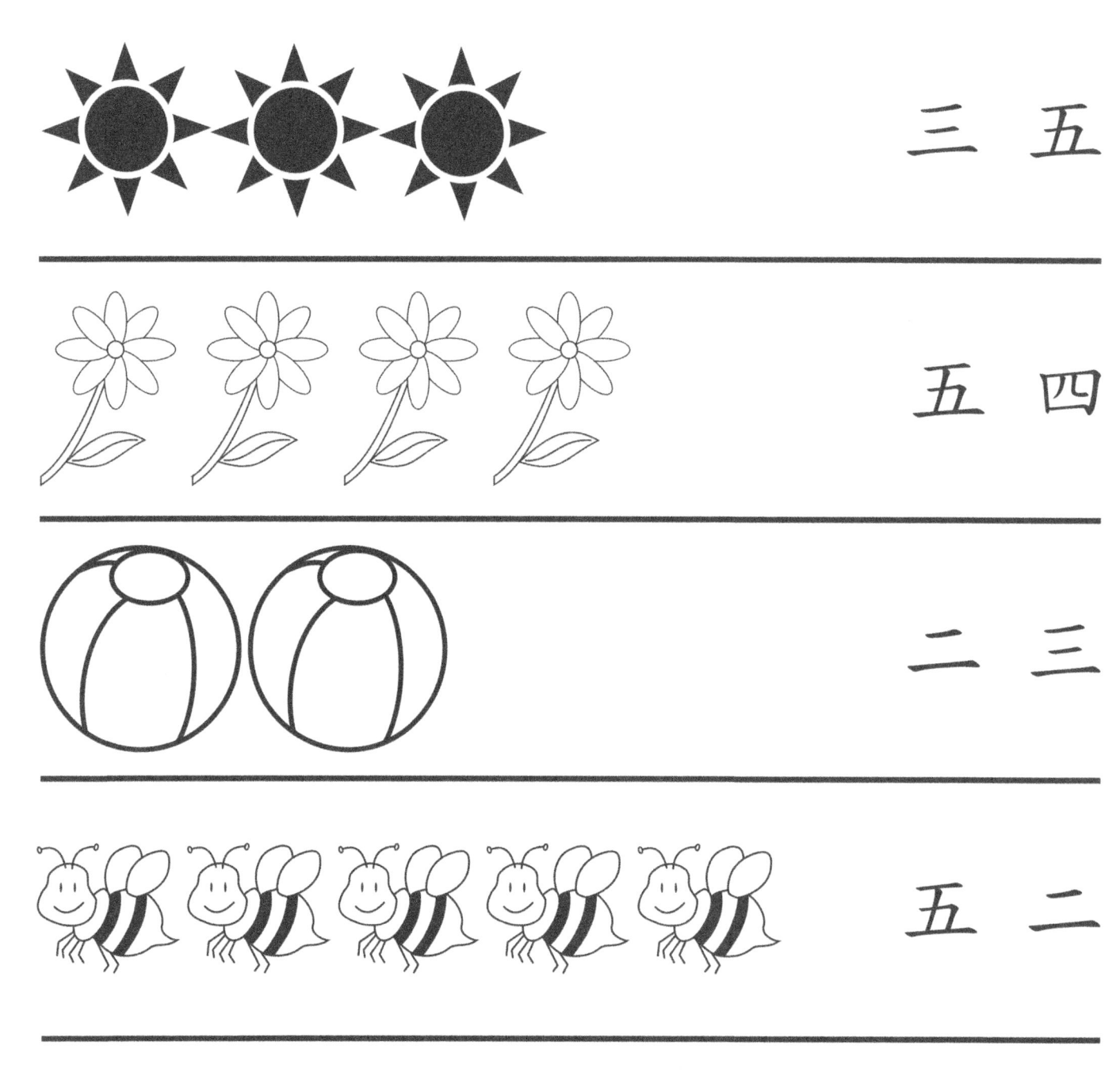

☀ ☀ ☀	三 五
🌼 🌼 🌼 🌼	五 四
⚽ ⚽	二 三
🐝 🐝 🐝 🐝 🐝	五 二
🧦	二 一

唸唸看
Read-Aloud

- 五個人在我家玩。
  There are five people playing in my house.

- 四隻白鳥在上頭。
  Four white birds are up there.

- 三隻花貓在下頭。
  Three multicolored cats are down there.

- 我說：「為什麼？」
  I say, "Why?"

- 媽媽說可以。
  Mom says yes.

恭喜你完成了這一課，請回到第一頁將本課的星星塗上顏色。
Congratulations! You have completed a lesson. Please color the star for this lesson on page 1.

第三課

Lesson 3 Dì – ground
De – structural particle (-ly)

本書中的國字筆順是依據中華民國教育部「常用國字標準字體筆順學習網」的筆劃順序彙編。
The stroke orders of the characters in this workbook follow the stroke orders provided on the "Learning Program for Stroke Order of Frequently Used Chinese Characters" website of the Ministry of Education, R.O.C. (Taiwan).

請將「地」字連到在地上跑的東西。
Connect the character 地 to things that run on the ground.

12

請將漁夫的釣桿畫上釣魚線連到有「地」字的魚並將牠著色。
Please draw a line from the fishing pole to the fish with the character 地 and color the fish.

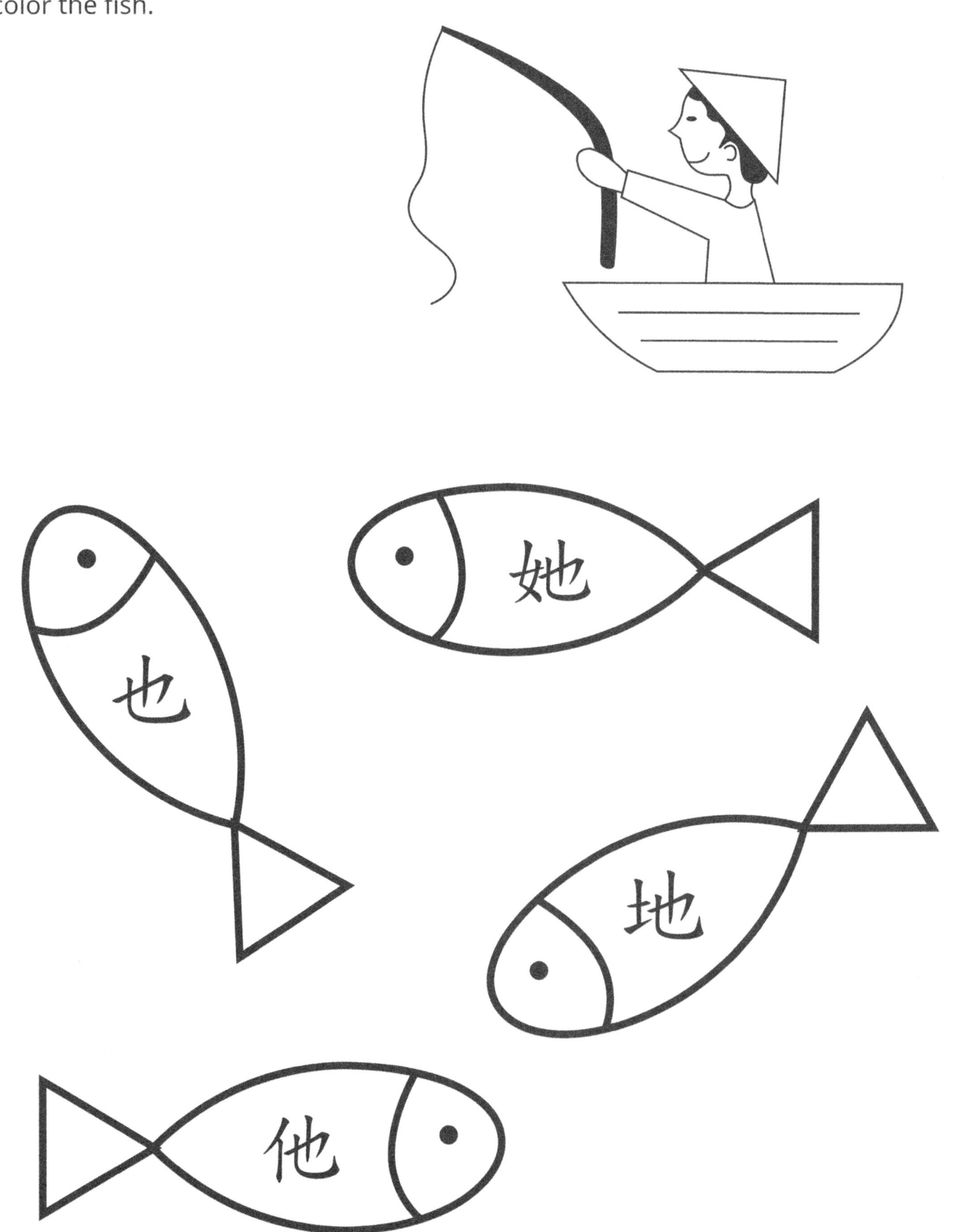

唸唸看
Read-Aloud

- 有什麼是在地下的？
  What things are underground?

- 小鳥不在地下。
  The little bird is not underground.

- 爸爸頭上有四隻小貓和五隻小鳥。
  There are four little cats and five little birds on Dad's head.

- 爸爸的頭很大。
  Dad's head is very big.

恭喜你完成了這一課，請回到第一頁將本課的星星塗上顏色。
Congratulations! You have completed a lesson. Please color the star for this lesson on page 1.

第四課

Lesson 4 Chū – go out; come out

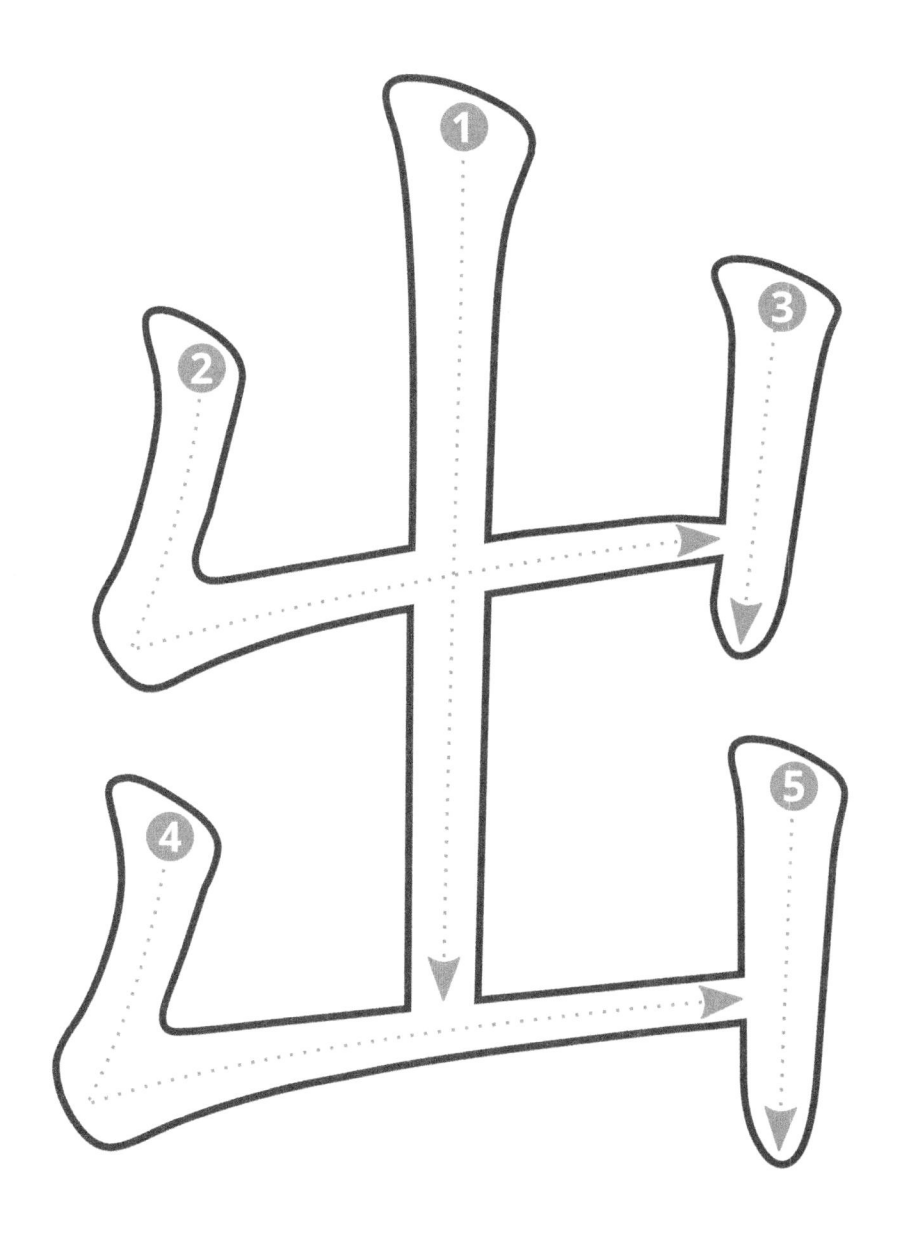

本書中的國字筆順是依據中華民國教育部「常用國字標準字體筆順學習網」的筆劃順序彙編。
The stroke orders of the characters in this workbook follow the stroke orders provided on the "Learning Program for Stroke Order of Frequently Used Chinese Characters" website of the Ministry of Education, R.O.C. (Taiwan).

跟著「出」字從 ➡ 到 ★ 走出迷宮。
Follow the characters 出 from the arrow to the star to exit the maze.

到	說	中	五	出
白	這	麼	什	出
好	為	地	出	出
出	出	出	出	山
出	五	以	也	四

16

找到「出」字圈出來。
Find the characters 出 and circle them.

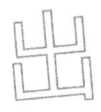

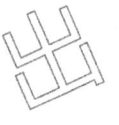

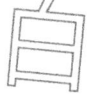

唸唸看
Read-Aloud

- 我們出去玩一下。

We go out and play a bit.

- 一、二、三、四、五。有五隻小鳥在花中。

One, two, three, four, five. There are five little birds in the flowers.

- 小鳥不想在地上。

The little bird does not want to be on the ground.

- 小貓說：「小鳥這麼好吃。」

The little cat says, "Little birds are so delicious."

恭喜你完成了這一課，請回到第一頁將本課的星星塗上顏色。

Congratulations! You have completed a lesson. Please color the star for this lesson on page 1.

第五課

Lesson 5 Tiān – sky

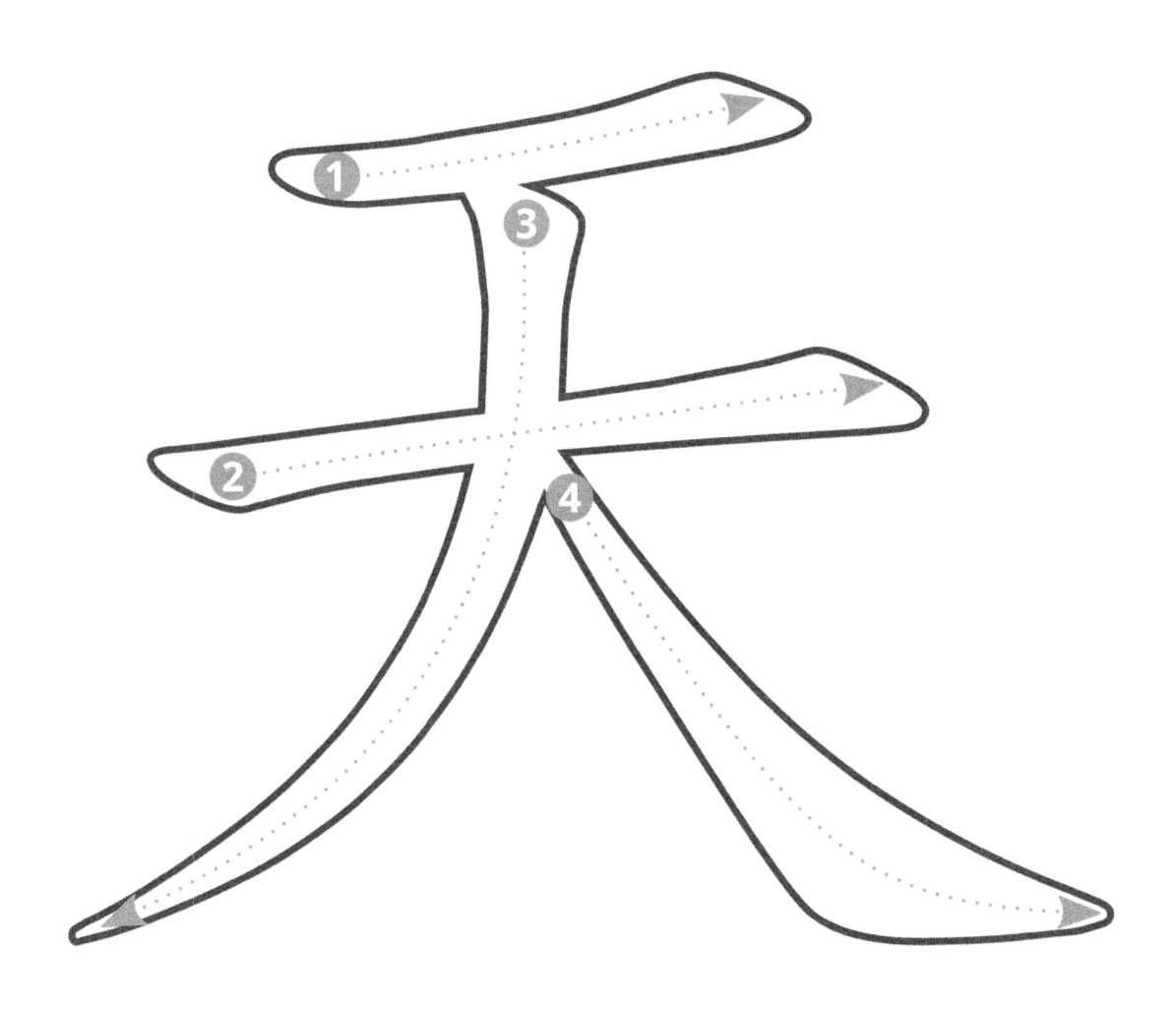

本書中的國字筆順是依據中華民國教育部「常用國字標準字體筆順學習網」的筆劃順序彙編。
The stroke orders of the characters in this workbook follow the stroke orders provided on the "Learning Program for Stroke Order of Frequently Used Chinese Characters" website of the Ministry of Education, R.O.C. (Taiwan).

「天」字是以大字表示人，上方的一橫則表示頭頂上的空間。
The character 天 uses the character 大 to represent a man, and the horizontal stroke above 大 represents the sky.

20

請將下方的圖案剪下來,將可在天上飛行的東西貼到「天」字下,不會飛的貼到「地」字下。

Paste the items that can fly under the character 天 and the items that cannot fly under the character 地.

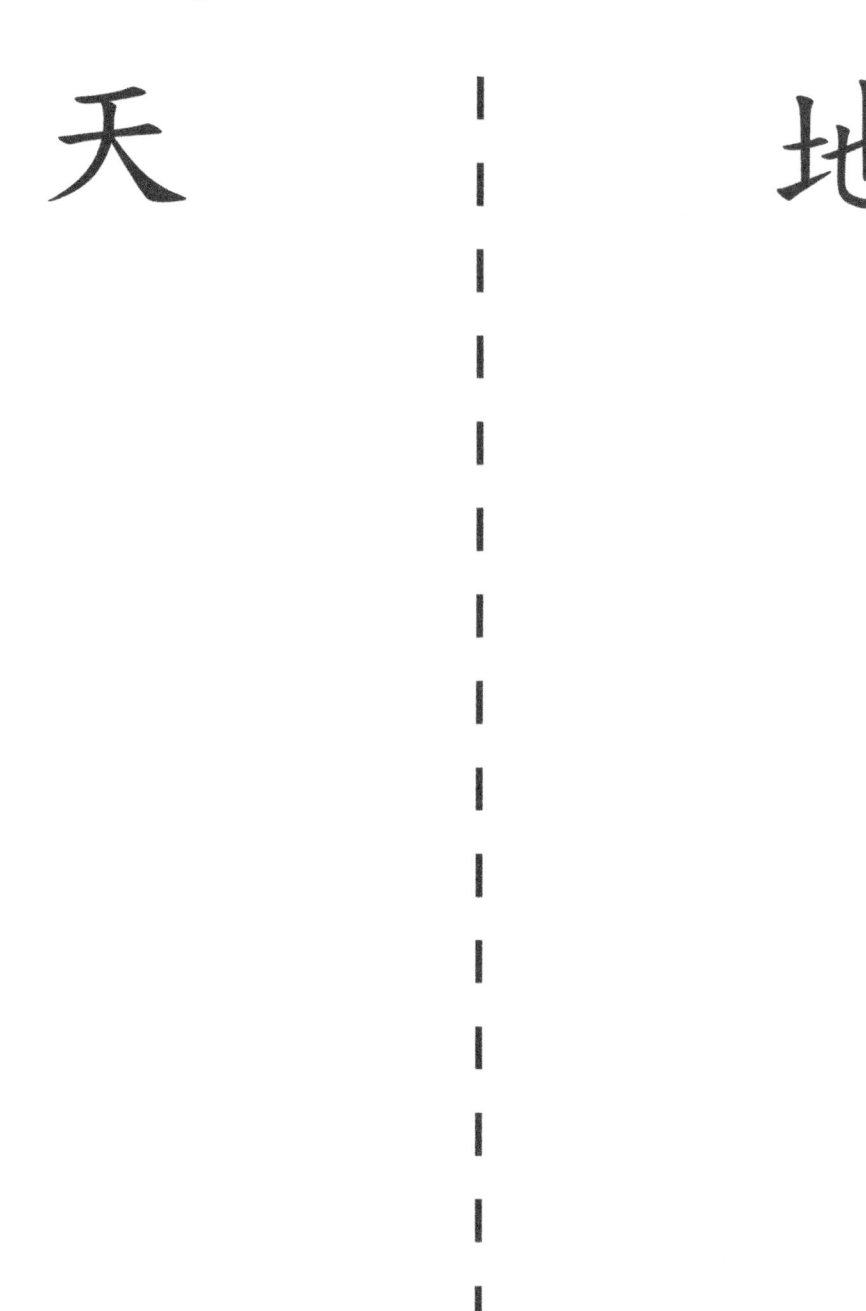

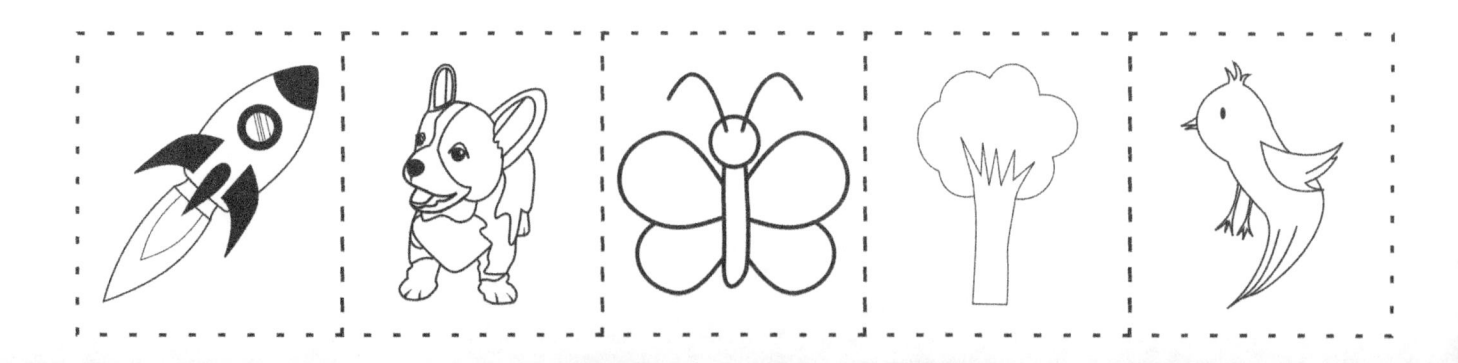

天　　　　｜　　　　地

唸唸看
Read-Aloud

- 四隻小白鳥在天上。
  Four little white birds are up in the sky.

- 五隻小花貓在地上。
  Five little multicolored cats are on the ground.

- 小貓們想一下吃了小鳥們。
  The little cats want to eat the little birds at once.

- 媽媽要小貓們回到家中。
  Mom wants the little cats to go back inside the house.

- 不要小貓們出去。
  (Mom) doesn't want the little cats to go out.

恭喜你完成了這一課,請回到第一頁將本課的星星塗上顏色。
Congratulations! You have completed a lesson. Please color the star for this lesson on page 1.

第六課

Lesson 6 Zǒu – walk; go

本書中的國字筆順是依據中華民國教育部「常用國字標準字體筆順學習網」的筆劃順序彙編。
The stroke orders of the characters in this workbook follow the stroke orders provided on the "Learning Program for Stroke Order of Frequently Used Chinese Characters" website of the Ministry of Education, R.O.C. (Taiwan).

將「走」字塗色，幫獅子回到樹下。
Color the characters 走 to find the path to the tree.

	走	走	走		什	
			走		下	
	起	走	走	去	四
	中		走		上
	五		走		
麼	以	出	走	走	
			天		

24

將有「走」字的葉子著色。
Color the leaves with the character 走.

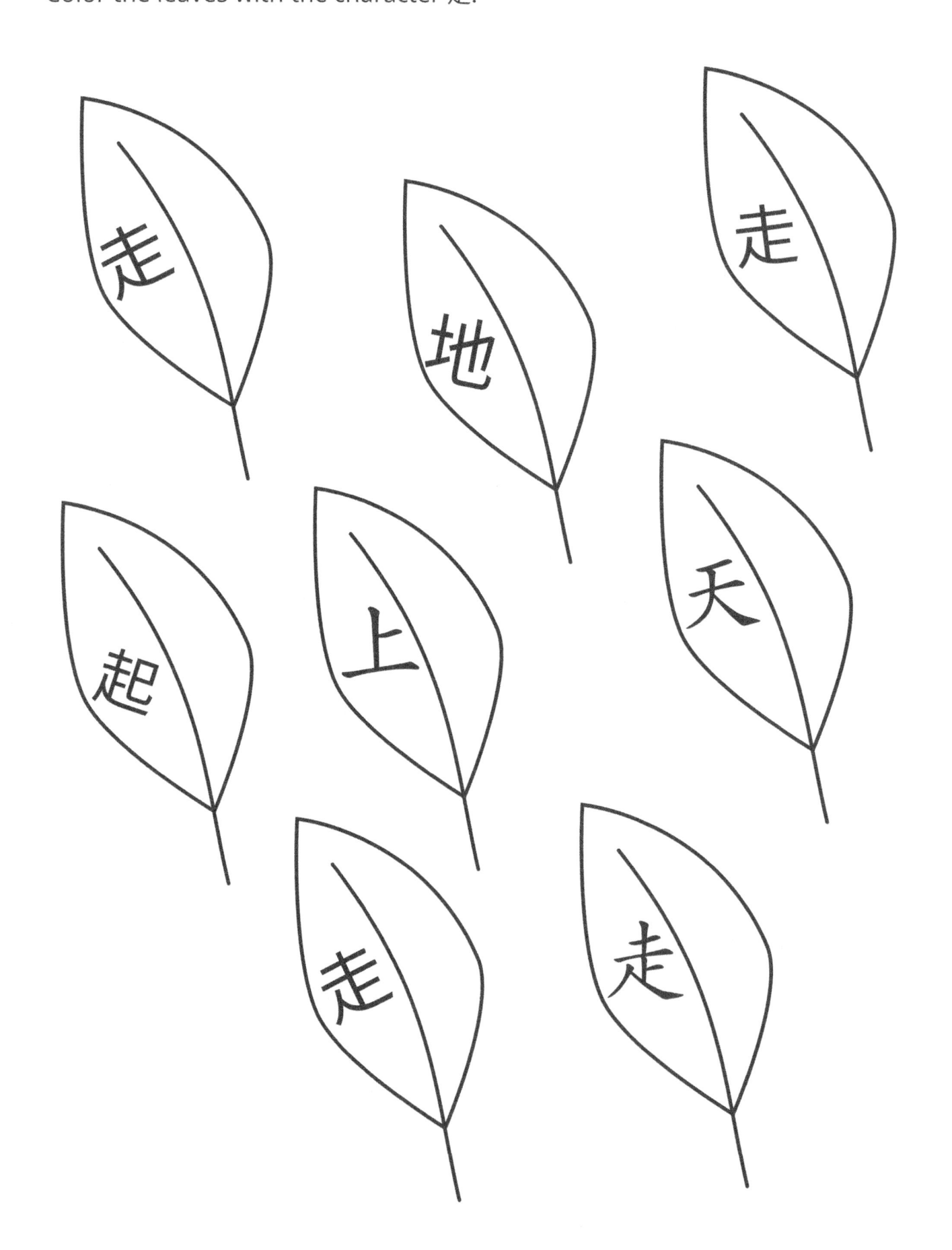

走　地　走
起　上　天
　　走　走

唸唸看
Read-Aloud

- 五隻小貓在地上走。
Five little cats are walking on the ground.

- 四隻小鳥在天上。
Four little birds are up in the sky.

- 大人說我們不可以出去。
The adults say we cannot go outside.

- 我們不愛在家玩。
We do not like to play at home.

- 我想要出去走走。
I want to go out for a walk.

恭喜你完成了這一課,請回到第一頁將本課的星星塗上顏色。
Congratulations! You have completed a lesson. Please color the star for this lesson on page 1.

第七課

Lesson 7 Hóng – red

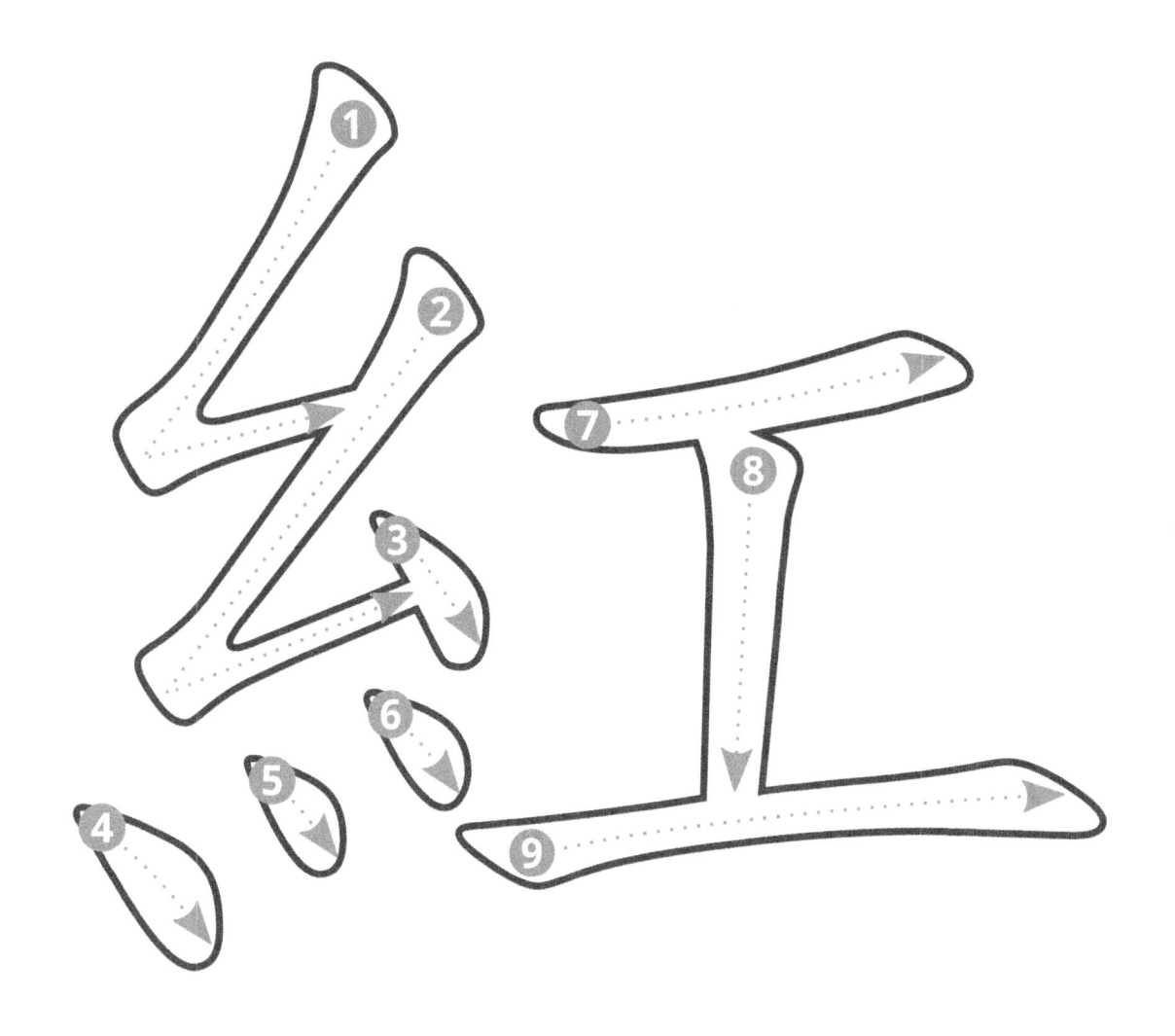

本書中的國字筆順是依據中華民國教育部「常用國字標準字體筆順學習網」的筆劃順序彙編。
The stroke orders of the characters in this workbook follow the stroke orders provided on the "Learning Program for Stroke Order of Frequently Used Chinese Characters" website of the Ministry of Education, R.O.C. (Taiwan).

請把花朵塗成紅色並唸出下面的文字。
Please color the flower red and read aloud the characters at the bottom.

紅花

請將有「紅」字的蘋果著色。
Please color the apples with the character 紅.

唸唸看
Read-Aloud

- 我頭上有五個大紅花。
  There are five big red flowers on my head.

- 我出去走走。
  I go out for a walk.

- 天上的小鳥下來了。
  The little bird in the sky came down.

- 小鳥到我的頭上了。
  The little bird landed on my head.

- 地上的小貓好想吃。
  The little cat on the ground wants to eat (it) so much.

恭喜你完成了這一課,請回到第一頁將本課的星星塗上顏色。
Congratulations! You have completed a lesson. Please color the star for this lesson on page 1.

第八課

Lesson 8 Tù – rabbit

本書中的國字筆順是依據中華民國教育部「常用國字標準字體筆順學習網」的筆劃順序彙編。
The stroke orders of the characters in this workbook follow the stroke orders provided on the "Learning Program for Stroke Order of Frequently Used Chinese Characters" website of the Ministry of Education, R.O.C. (Taiwan).

找出到達「兔」字的路。
Find the path leading to the character 兔.

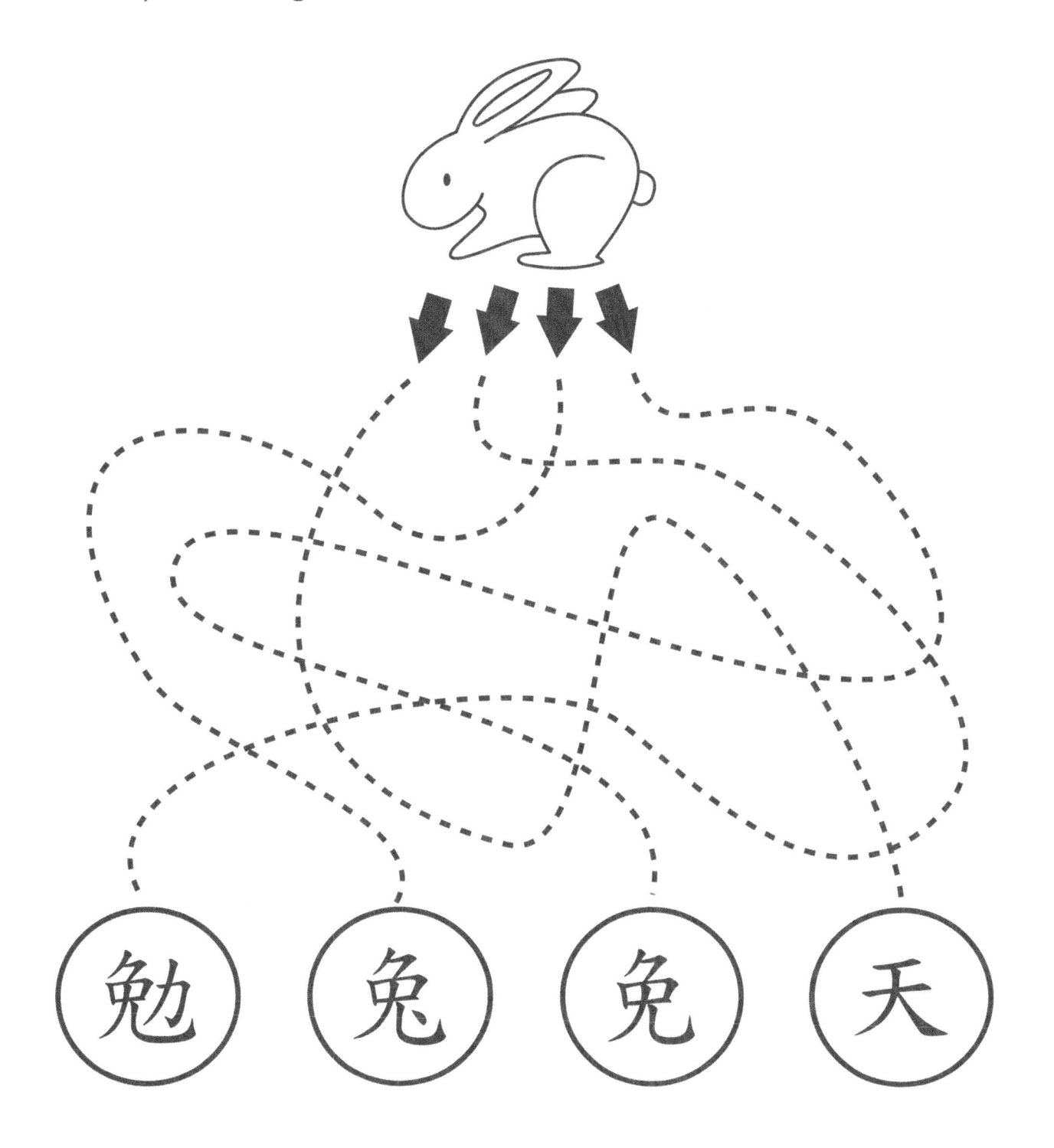

32

請將下方的圖案剪下來讓孩子貼在正確的文字上。
Please cut out the picture blocks below and paste them to the correct character boxes.

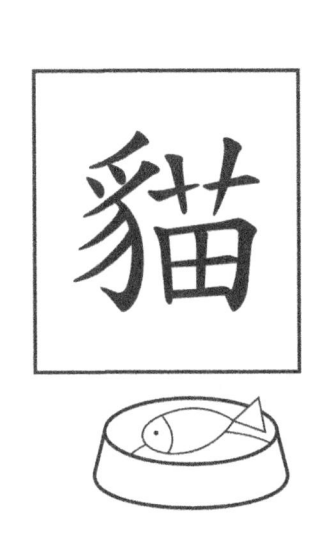

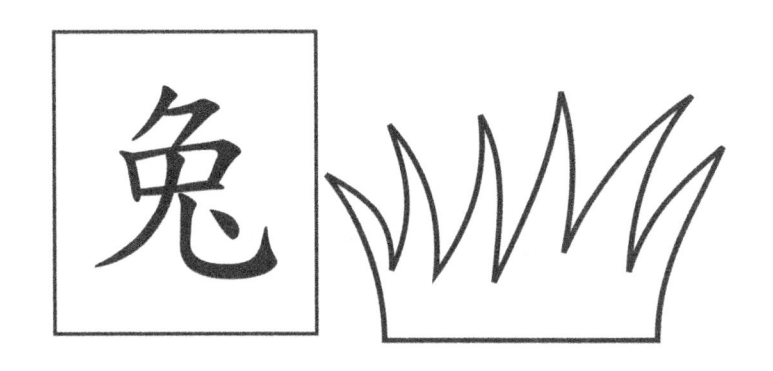

貓

鳥

兔

唸唸看
Read-Aloud

- 地上有一隻小白兔。
  There is a little white rabbit on the ground.

- 小白兔走出來吃紅花。
  The little white rabbit comes out to eat red flowers.

- 小花貓愛吃天上的小鳥和地上的小白兔。
  The little multicolored cat likes to eat the little bird in the sky and the little white rabbit on the ground.

- 媽媽和小貓說:「不可以。」
  Mom told the little cat, "No."

恭喜你完成了這一課,請回到第一頁將本課的星星塗上顏色。
Congratulations! You have completed a lesson. Please color the star for this lesson on page 1.

第九課

Lesson 9 Jiù – just (emphasis); at once; right away

本書中的國字筆順是依據中華民國教育部「常用國字標準字體筆順學習網」的筆劃順序彙編。
The stroke orders of the characters in this workbook follow the stroke orders provided on the "Learning Program for Stroke Order of Frequently Used Chinese Characters" website of the Ministry of Education, R.O.C. (Taiwan).

跟著「就」字從 ➡ 到 ★ 走出迷宮。
Follow the characters 就 from the arrow to the star to exit the maze.

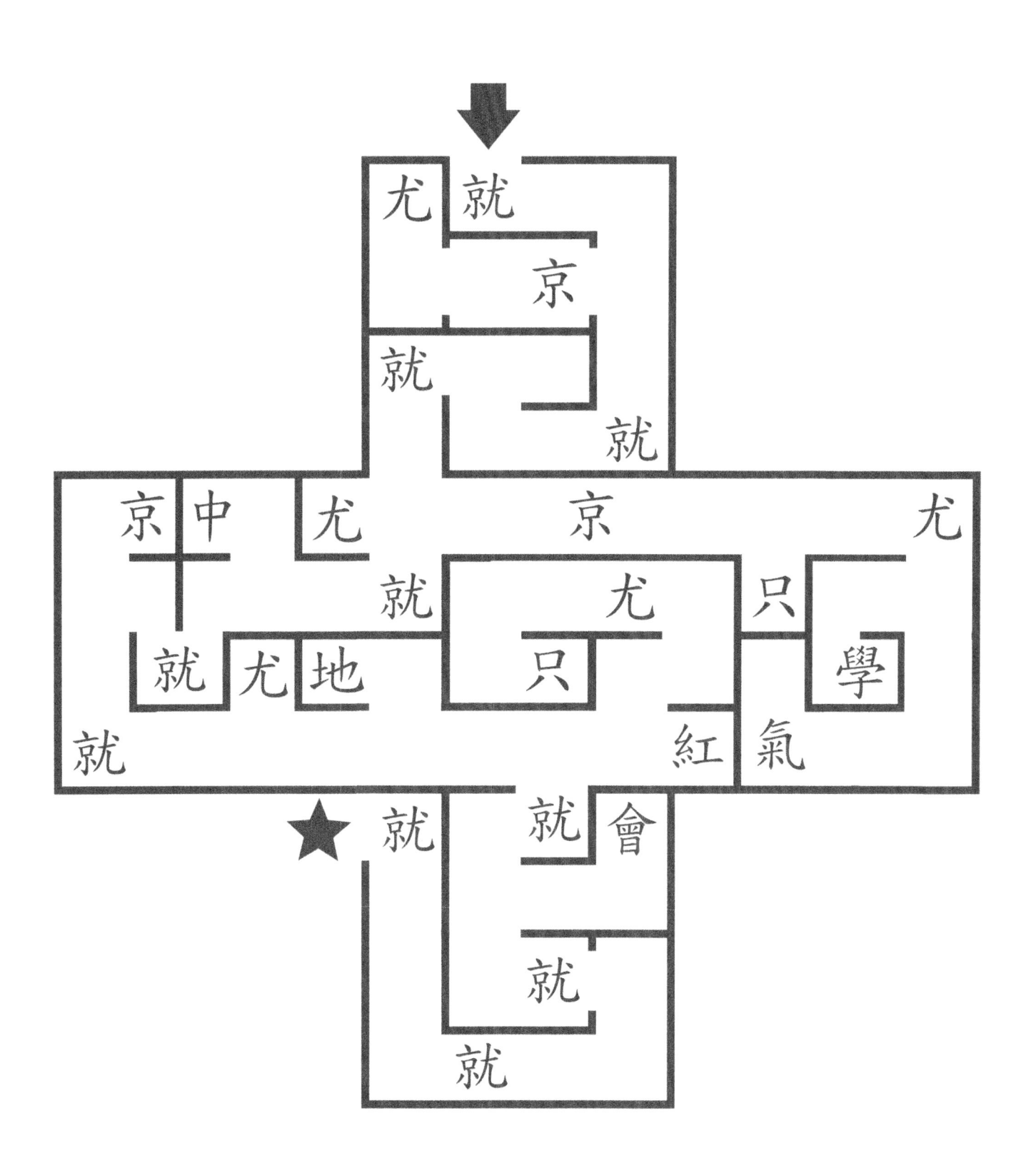

連連看一樣的字。
Draw lines to connect the matching characters.

就 •　　　　　• 兔

紅 •　　　　　• 紅

兔 •　　　　　• 走

走 •　　　　　• 就

唸唸看
Read-Aloud

- 小貓為什麼想要吃天上的小鳥和地上的小白兔？
  Why does the little cat want to eat the little bird in the sky and the little white rabbit on the ground?

- 小貓就是愛吃。
  The little cat just loves to eat (them).

- 小貓走出去了。
  The little cat walked outside.

- 小白兔在吃紅花。
  The little white rabbit is eating red flowers.

恭喜你完成了這一課，請回到第一頁將本課的星星塗上顏色。
Congratulations! You have completed a lesson. Please color the star for this lesson on page 1.

第十課

Lesson 10 Kàn – look; see

本書中的國字筆順是依據中華民國教育部「常用國字標準字體筆順學習網」的筆劃順序彙編。
The stroke orders of the characters in this workbook follow the stroke orders provided on the "Learning Program for Stroke Order of Frequently Used Chinese Characters" website of the Ministry of Education, R.O.C. (Taiwan).

「看」字就像把手放在眼睛上方望向遠處的樣子。請將下圖著色。
The character 看 is like a hand shading the eye to look far away. Please color the picture below.

40

請將有「看」字的地方著色。
Color the areas with the character 看.

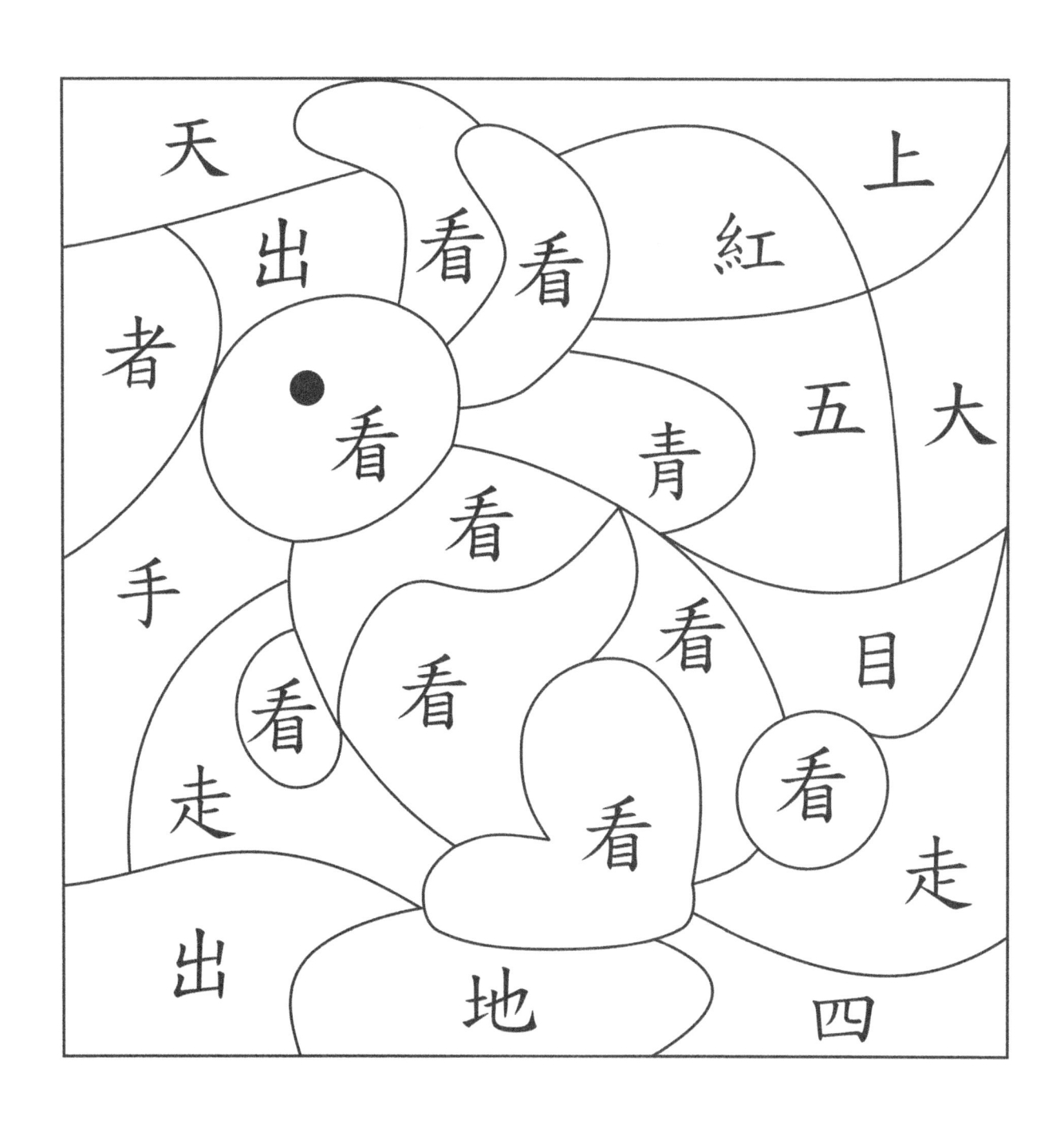

唸唸看
Read-Aloud

- 小花貓一看到小白兔就走出去了。

The little multicolored cat walked outside as soon as it saw the little white rabbit.

- 天上的小紅鳥一看到小花貓就不下來了。

The little red bird in the sky did not come down when it saw the little multicolored cat.

- 我和媽媽一起和小貓說：「不可以。」

Mom and I told the little multicolored cat together, "No."

恭喜你完成了這一課，請回到第一頁將本課的星星塗上顏色。
Congratulations! You have completed a lesson. Please color the star for this lesson on page 1.

第十一課

Lesson 11 Qì – air; weather; to get/make angry

本書中的國字筆順是依據中華民國教育部「常用國字標準字體筆順學習網」的筆劃順序彙編。
The stroke orders of the characters in this workbook follow the stroke orders provided on the "Learning Program for Stroke Order of Frequently Used Chinese Characters" website of the Ministry of Education, R.O.C. (Taiwan).

把有「氣」字的氣球著色並且連到小孩手中。
Color the balloons with the character 氣 and connect them to the child.

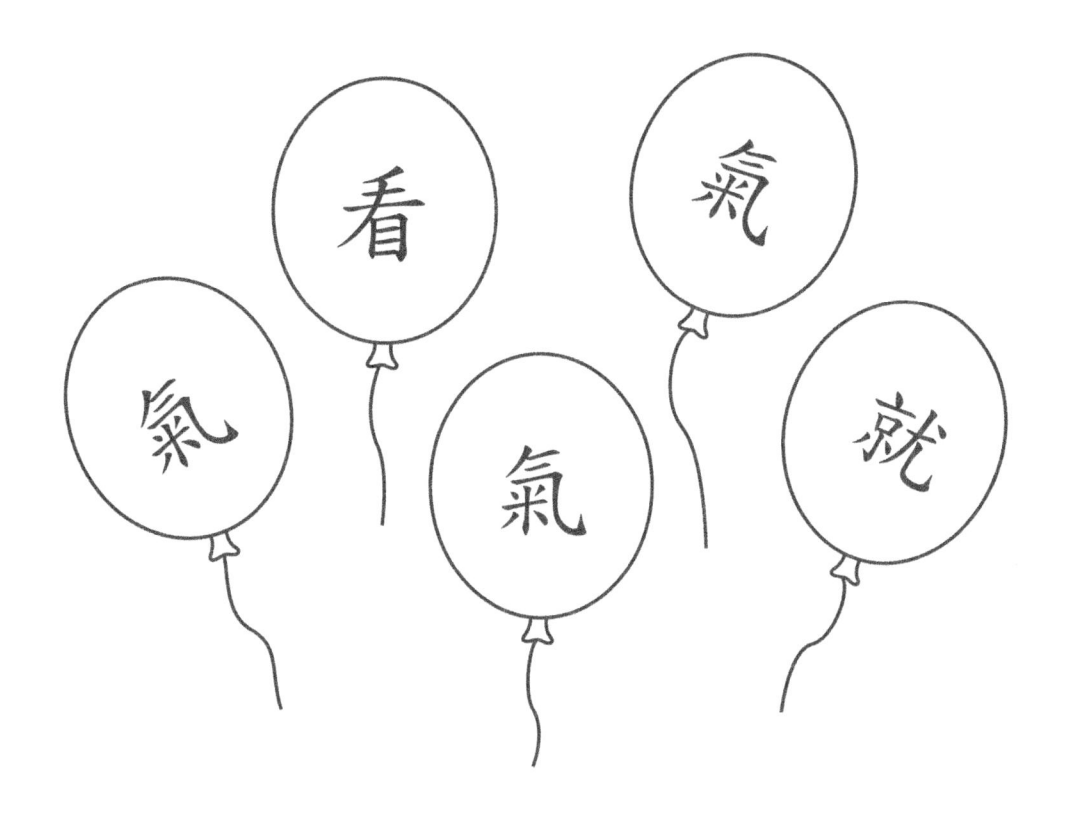

44

找到「氣」字圈出來。
Find the characters 氣 and circle them.

氣　　　氣　　天

　　看

　汽　　　　　氣

　　　米

　紅　　羊　　氣

　　　　　出

　　就

唸唸看
Read-Aloud

- 天氣好我們就出去走走。
  (If) the weather is good, we will go out for a walk.

- 我們看到地上有紅花，天上有鳥。
  We see there are red flowers on the ground, (and) birds in the sky.

- 小貓看到地上有小白兔。
  The little cat sees there is (a) little white rabbit on the ground.

- 媽媽說：「不可以。」
  Mom says, "No."

- 小貓好氣。
  The little cat is very angry.

恭喜你完成了這一課，請回到第一頁將本課的星星塗上顏色。
Congratulations! You have completed a lesson. Please color the star for this lesson on page 1.

第十二課

Lesson 12 Shēng – to be born; to give birth; raw; student

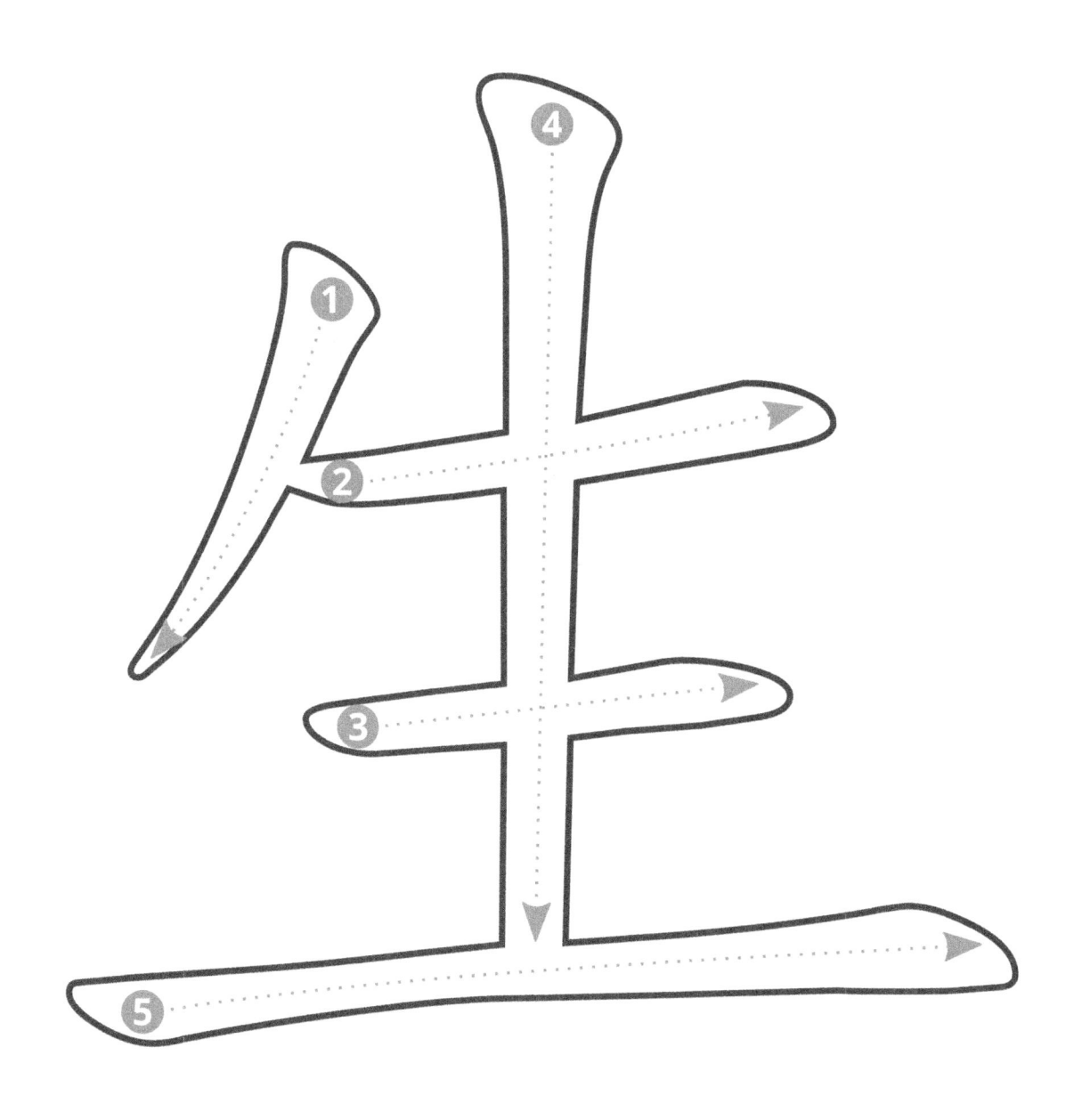

本書中的國字筆順是依據中華民國教育部「常用國字標準字體筆順學習網」的筆劃順序彙編。
The stroke orders of the characters in this workbook follow the stroke orders provided on the "Learning Program for Stroke Order of Frequently Used Chinese Characters" website of the Ministry of Education, R.O.C. (Taiwan).

跟著「生」字從 ➡ 到 ★ 走出迷宮。
Follow the characters 生 from the arrow to the star to exit the maze.

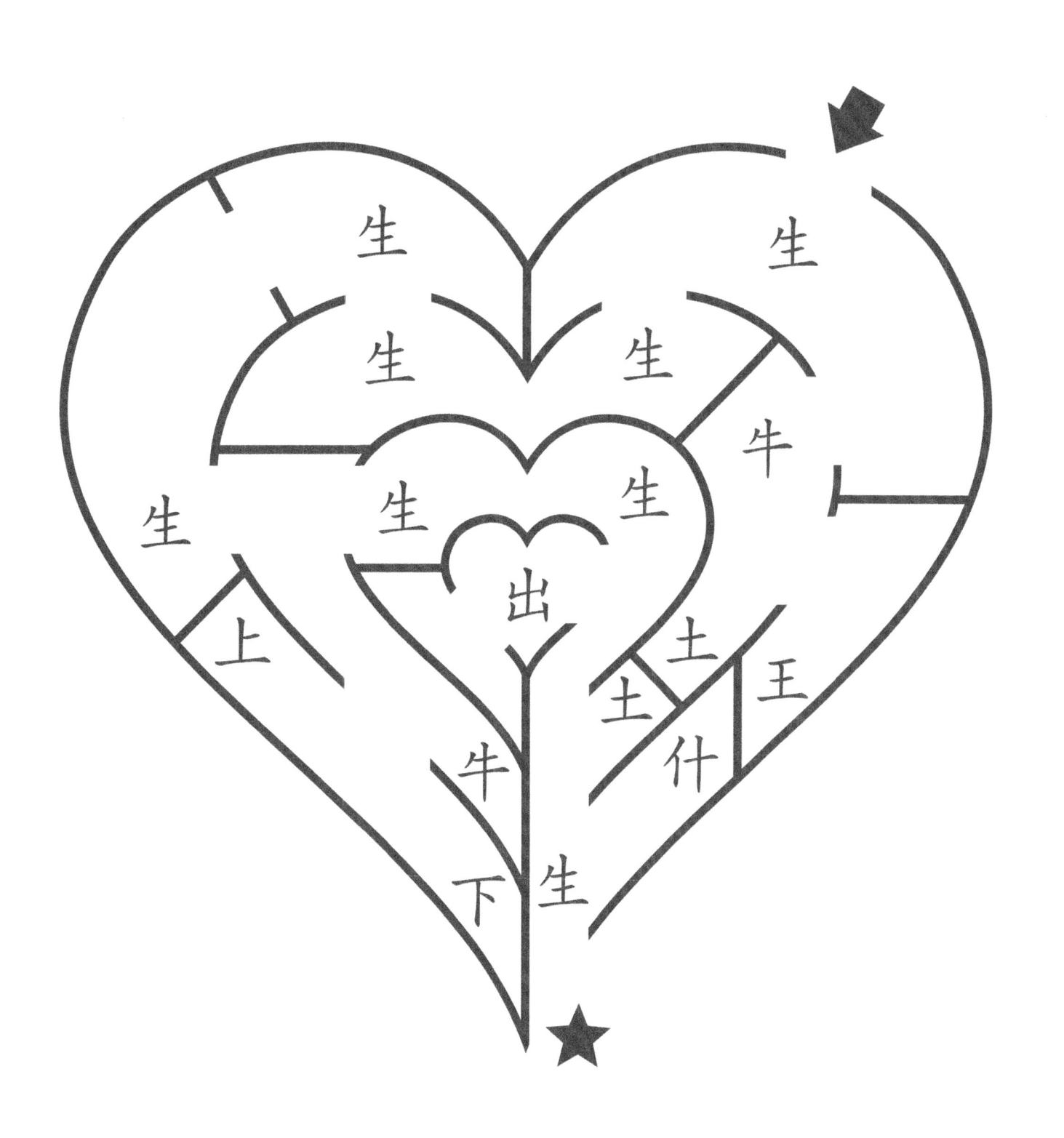

48

將「生」字塗色，幫助小老鼠找到乳酪。
Color the characters 生 to help the mouse find the path to the cheese.

唸唸看
Read-Aloud

- 小貓是在我們家出生的。
The little cat was born in our house.

- 小貓一看到小白兔就想要吃。
The little cat wants to eat the little white rabbit as soon as it sees it.

- 小貓不可以吃小白兔。
The little cat cannot eat the little white rabbit.

- 小貓很生氣。
The little cat is very angry.

- 小貓氣紅了,好可愛。
The little cat turned red from anger, (it is) so cute.

恭喜你完成了這一課,請回到第一頁將本課的星星塗上顏色。
Congratulations! You have completed a lesson. Please color the star for this lesson on page 1.

第十三課

Lesson 13 Xué – learn; imitate

本書中的國字筆順是依據中華民國教育部「常用國字標準字體筆順學習網」的筆劃順序彙編。
The stroke orders of the characters in this workbook follow the stroke orders provided on the "Learning Program for Stroke Order of Frequently Used Chinese Characters" website of the Ministry of Education, R.O.C. (Taiwan).

跟著「學」字從 ➡ 到 ★ 走出迷宮。
Follow the characters 學 from the arrow to the star to exit the maze.

走	就	覺	學	學
氣	愛	學	學	看
兔	覺	學	覺	媽
學	學	學	五	四
學	氣	走	的	出

52

請將下方的字格剪下來選擇正確的字貼上。
Please cut out the characters at the bottom and paste the correct ones.

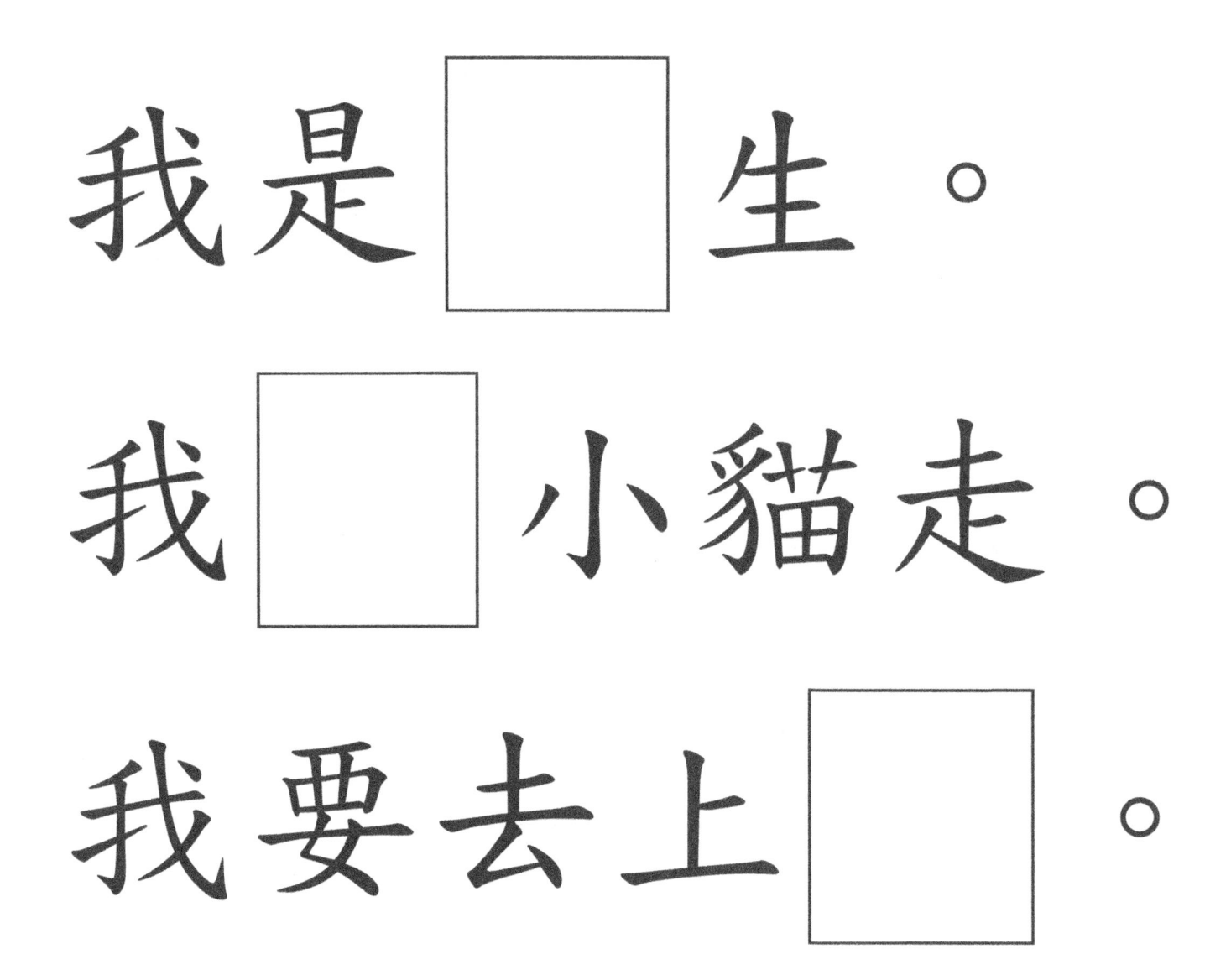

我是☐生。

我☐小貓走。

我要去上☐。

| 學 | 覺 | 學 | 覺 | 學 |

唸唸看
Read-Aloud

- 我是一個學生。
I am a student.

- 我一看到小貓，我就學貓走。
When I see a little cat, I imitate the cat walking.

- 我學小貓生氣。
I imitate the cat getting angry.

- 我也學兔子吃紅花。
I also imitate the rabbit eating red flowers.

- 媽媽說：「為什麼要學？」
Mom says, "Why (are you) imitating?"

恭喜你完成了這一課，請回到第一頁將本課的星星塗上顏色。
Congratulations! You have completed a lesson. Please color the star for this lesson on page 1.

第十四課

Lesson 14 Tiào – jump; hop

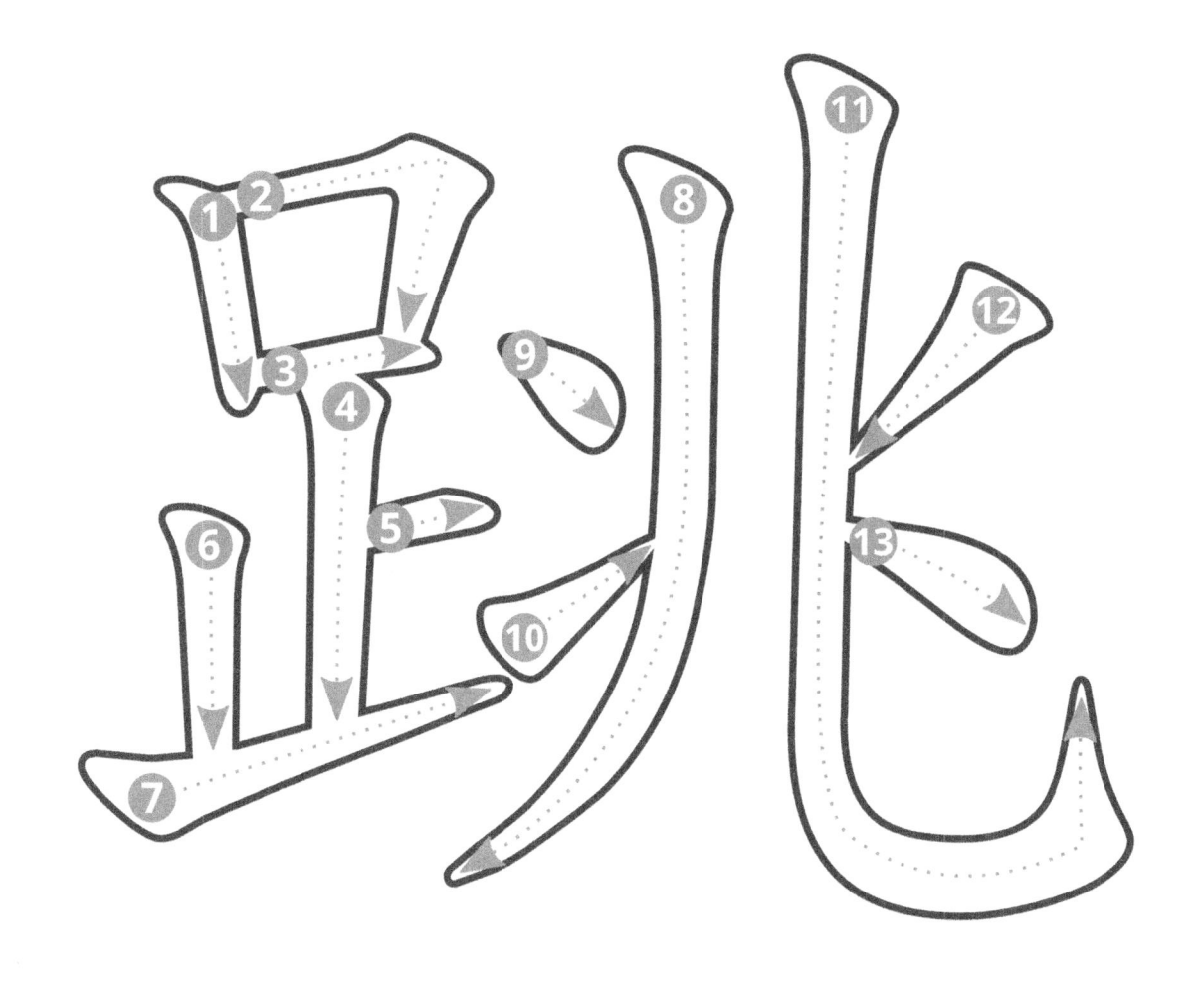

本書中的國字筆順是依據中華民國教育部「常用國字標準字體筆順學習網」的筆劃順序彙編。
The stroke orders of the characters in this workbook follow the stroke orders provided on the "Learning Program for Stroke Order of Frequently Used Chinese Characters" website of the Ministry of Education, R.O.C. (Taiwan).

請將文字連到對應的圖案。
Connect the characters to the correct pictures.

走 •

跳 •

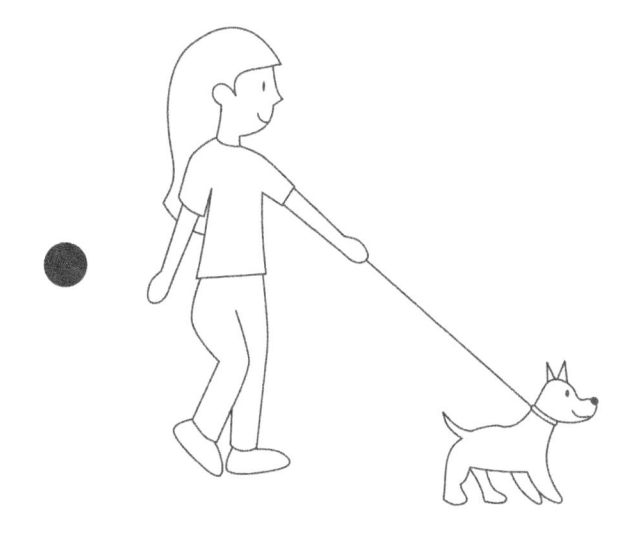

請把「跳」字連到正確的圖案。
Please connect the character 跳 to the correct picture.

唸唸看
Read-Aloud

- 小白兔就是想要跳。
The little white rabbit just wants to hop.

- 我是一個學生。
I am a student.

- 我們愛好天氣。
We love good weather.

- 天氣好就可以一起出去走走。
If the weather is good, (we) can go outside together for a walk.

恭喜你完成了這一課,請回到第一頁將本課的星星塗上顏色。
Congratulations! You have completed a lesson. Please color the star for this lesson on page 1.

第十五課

Lesson 15 Fēi – fly

本書中的國字筆順是依據中華民國教育部「常用國字標準字體筆順學習網」的筆劃順序彙編。
The stroke orders of the characters in this workbook follow the stroke orders provided on the "Learning Program for Stroke Order of Frequently Used Chinese Characters" website of the Ministry of Education, R.O.C. (Taiwan).

请將有「飛」字的地方著色並唸出下方的文字。
Color the areas with the character 飛 and read aloud the characters at the bottom.

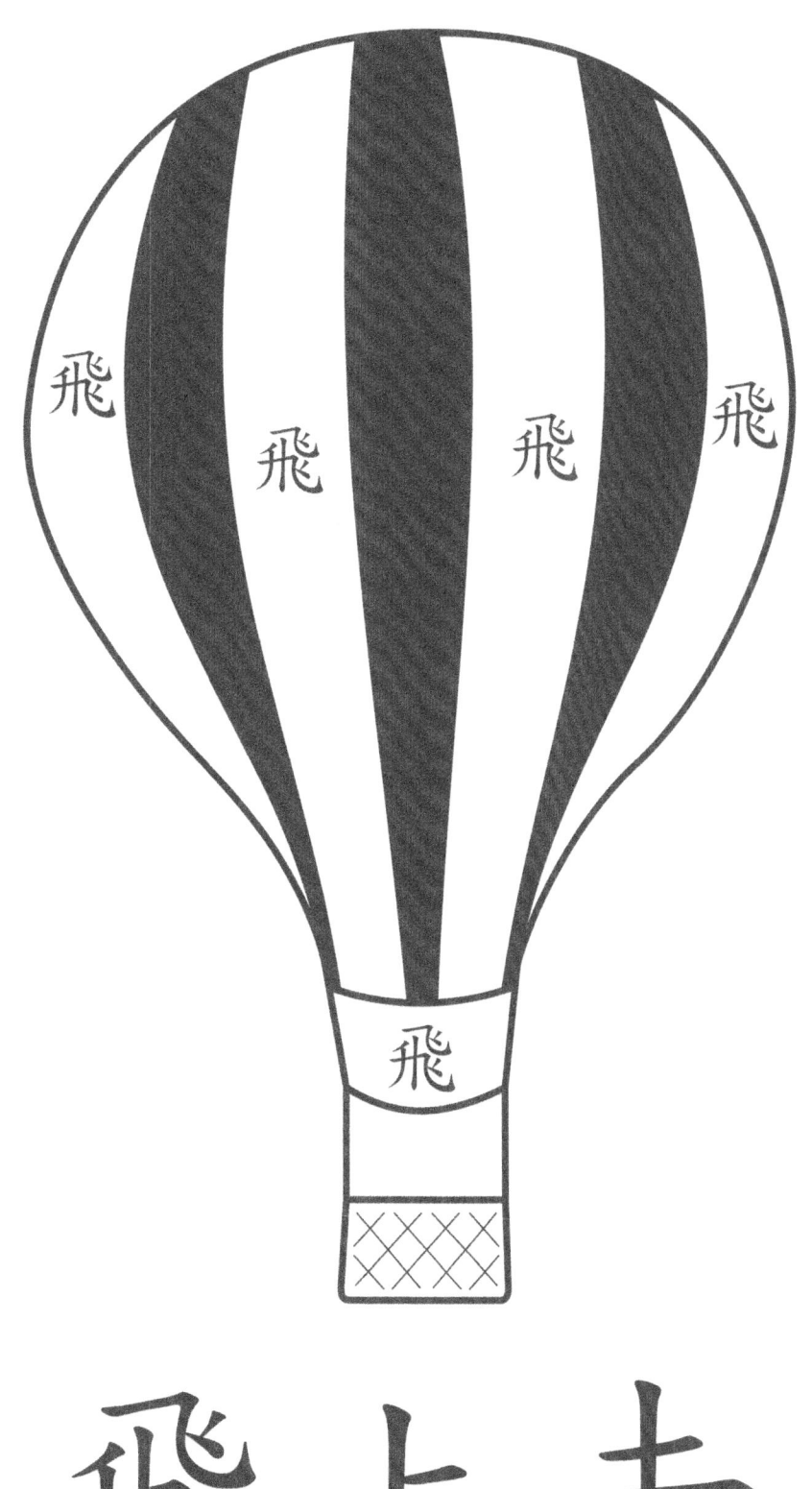

飛上去

把會飛的東西連到「飛」字。
Connect the character 飛 to the things that fly.

飛

唸唸看
Read-Aloud

- 四隻小鳥在天上飛。
Four little birds are flying in the sky.

- 小貓生氣地跳起來。
The little cat angrily jumps up.

- 小貓說:「為什麼小鳥不下來?」
The little cat says, "Why doesn't the little bird come down?"

- 小鳥看到了不下來。
The little bird sees (the little cat) and doesn't come down.

- 小貓愛吃小鳥。
The little cat loves to eat little birds.

恭喜你完成了這一課,請回到第一頁將本課的星星塗上顏色。
Congratulations! You have completed a lesson. Please color the star for this lesson on page 1.

第十六課

Lesson 16 Huì – can; to be able to; to meet

本書中的國字筆順是依據中華民國教育部「常用國字標準字體筆順學習網」的筆劃順序彙編。
The stroke orders of the characters in this workbook follow the stroke orders provided on the "Learning Program for Stroke Order of Frequently Used Chinese Characters" website of the Ministry of Education, R.O.C. (Taiwan).

將有「會」字的花瓶著色。
Color the vases with the character 會.

會	曾	會
繪	會	檜
薈	會	儈

63

64

將下方的字格剪下來讓孩子貼在會做的事情旁。
Cut out the character blocks below and paste them next to tasks that you can do.

會　會　會　會　會

唸唸看
Read-Aloud

- 小鳥會在天上飛。
Little birds can fly in the sky.

- 我和小貓不會飛。
The little cat and I cannot fly.

- 小鳥沒有在地上走。
The little bird is not walking on the ground.

- 小貓一看到小鳥在天上就很生氣。
When the little cat sees the little bird in the sky, (it) gets very angry.

- 可是小貓學不會飛。
But the little cat cannot learn to fly.

恭喜你完成了這一課，請回到第一頁將本課的星星塗上顏色。
Congratulations! You have completed a lesson. Please color the star for this lesson on page 1.

第十七課

Lesson 17 Lán – blue

本書中的國字筆順是依據中華民國教育部「常用國字標準字體筆順學習網」的筆劃順序彙編。
The stroke orders of the characters in this workbook follow the stroke orders provided on the "Learning Program for Stroke Order of Frequently Used Chinese Characters" website of the Ministry of Education, R.O.C. (Taiwan).

請將旗子塗上裡面所寫的顏色。
Please color the flags with the indicated color.

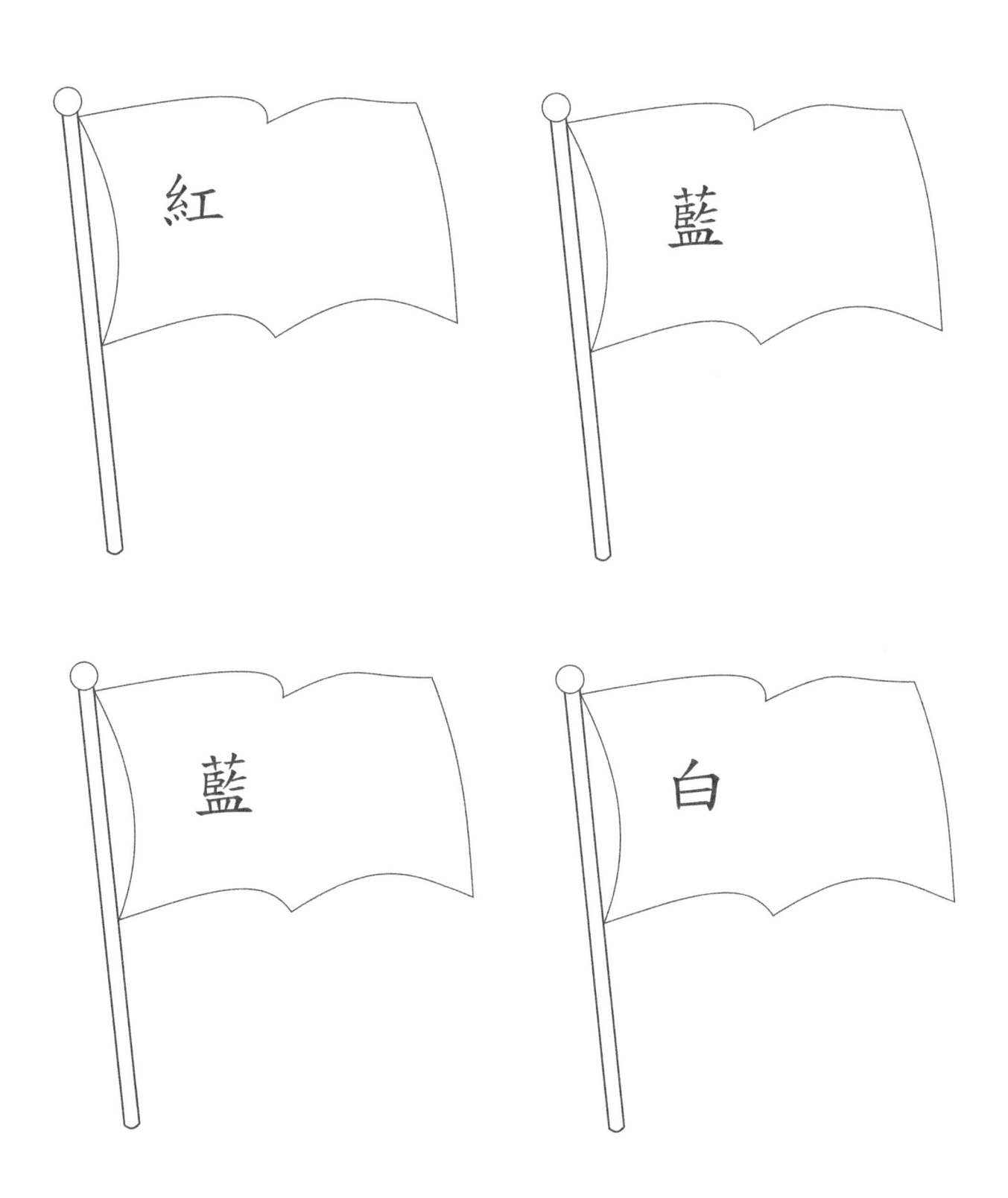

紅

藍

藍

白

找出「藍」字圈出來。
Find the characters 藍 and circle them.

學　飛　跳　藍

監

藍　藍　會

鹽　氣

唸唸看
Read-Aloud

- 小鳥會在藍天上飛。
Little birds can fly in the blue sky.

- 白兔會在地上跳。
White rabbits can hop on the ground.

- 我會學白兔跳。
I can imitate white rabbits hopping.

- 地上沒有藍的花。
There are no blue flowers on the ground.

- 小白兔好生氣。
The little white rabbit is very angry.

恭喜你完成了這一課,請回到第一頁將本課的星星塗上顏色。
Congratulations! You have completed a lesson. Please color the star for this lesson on page 1.

第十八課

Lesson 18 Tā – he; him

本書中的國字筆順是依據中華民國教育部「常用國字標準字體筆順學習網」的筆劃順序彙編。
The stroke orders of the characters in this workbook follow the stroke orders provided on the "Learning Program for Stroke Order of Frequently Used Chinese Characters" website of the Ministry of Education, R.O.C. (Taiwan).

請將下方的字格剪下來讓孩子選擇正確的字貼上。
Please cut out the characters at the bottom and paste the correct one.

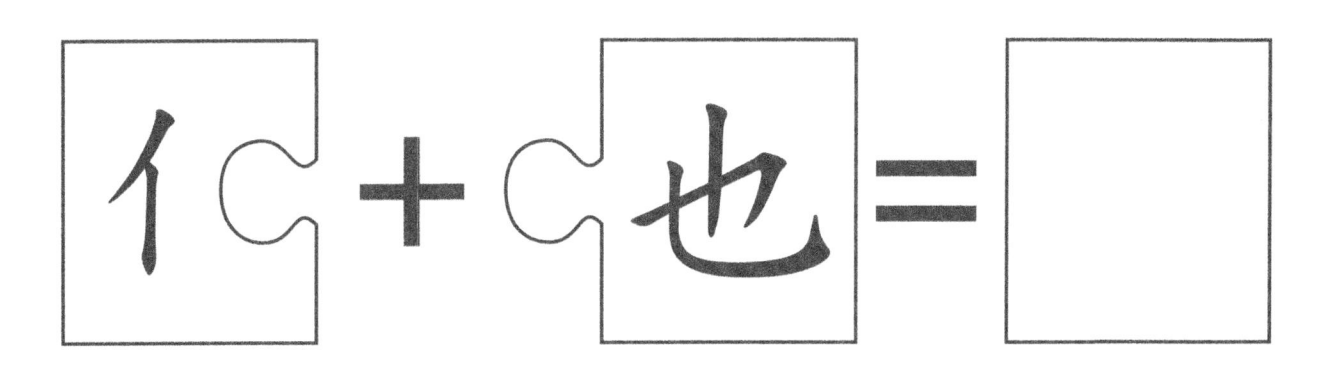

亻 + 也 = ☐

亻 也 他 她 地

連連看一樣的字。
Draw lines to connect the matching characters.

你 •　　　　　• 我

我 •　　　　　• 他

他 •　　　　　• 你

唸唸看
Read-Aloud

- 他是一隻可愛的小鳥。
  He is a cute little bird.

- 他會在藍藍的天上飛。
  He can fly in the blue sky.

- 你是一隻可愛的白兔。
  You are a cute white rabbit.

- 你會在地上跳。
  You can hop on the ground.

- 我們學不會飛。
  We cannot learn to fly.

恭喜你完成了這一課,請回到第一頁將本課的星星塗上顏色。
Congratulations! You have completed a lesson. Please color the star for this lesson on page 1.

第十九課

Lesson 19 Míng – bright; clear; understand

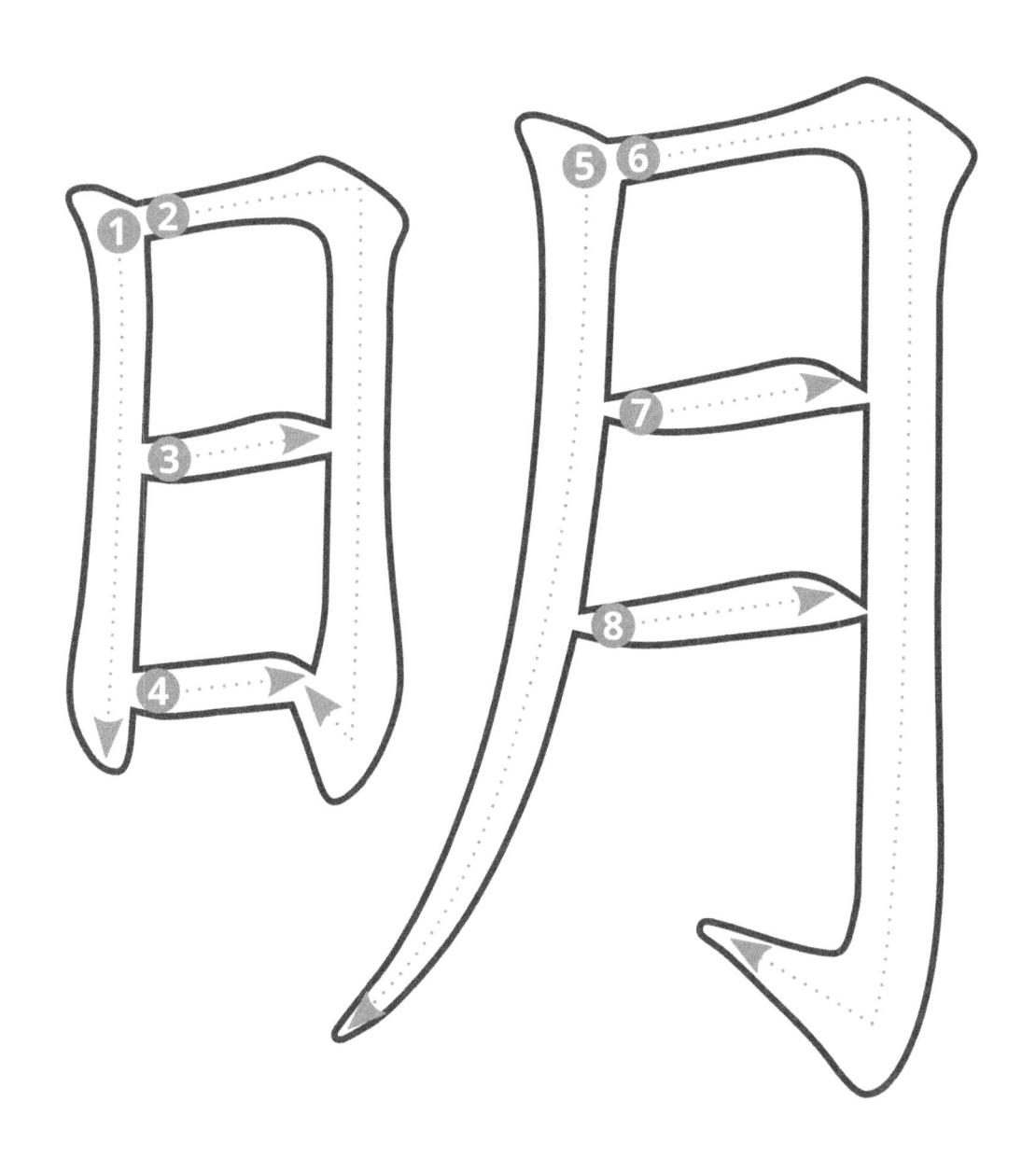

本書中的國字筆順是依據中華民國教育部「常用國字標準字體筆順學習網」的筆劃順序彙編。
The stroke orders of the characters in this workbook follow the stroke orders provided on the "Learning Program for Stroke Order of Frequently Used Chinese Characters" website of the Ministry of Education, R.O.C. (Taiwan).

「明」字是用太陽和月亮來表示日光或月光將空間照亮。請將下圖著色。
The character 明 is depicted by a sun and a moon meaning bright. Please color the image below.

76

請將下方的字格剪下來讓孩子選擇正確的字貼上。
Please cut out the characters at the bottom and paste the correct one.

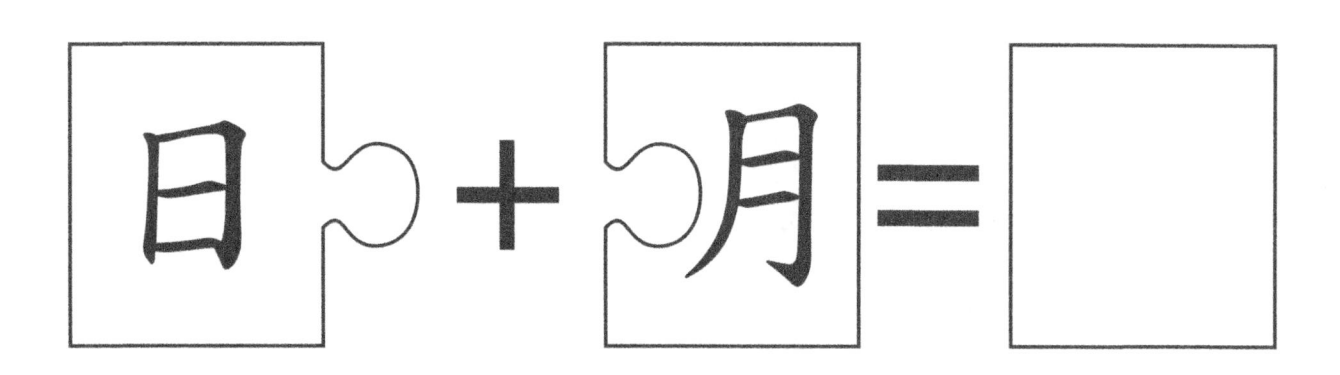

日 + 月 = ☐

| 日 | 月 | 有 | 朋 | 明 |

唸唸看
Read-Aloud

- 明天他會出去看看小鳥。
Tomorrow he will go out to see the little bird.

- 小鳥會飛也會跳。
The little bird can fly and hop.

- 他明明很愛小鳥。
He clearly loves the little bird very much.

- 可是小鳥不愛他。
But the little bird does not love him.

- 小鳥愛在藍天上飛。
The little bird loves to fly in the blue sky.

恭喜你完成了這一課，請回到第一頁將本課的星星塗上顏色。
Congratulations! You have completed a lesson. Please color the star for this lesson on page 1.

第二十課

Lesson 20 Zhǐ – only; just

本書中的國字筆順是依據中華民國教育部「常用國字標準字體筆順學習網」的筆劃順序彙編。
The stroke orders of the characters in this workbook follow the stroke orders provided on the "Learning Program for Stroke Order of Frequently Used Chinese Characters" website of the Ministry of Education, R.O.C. (Taiwan).

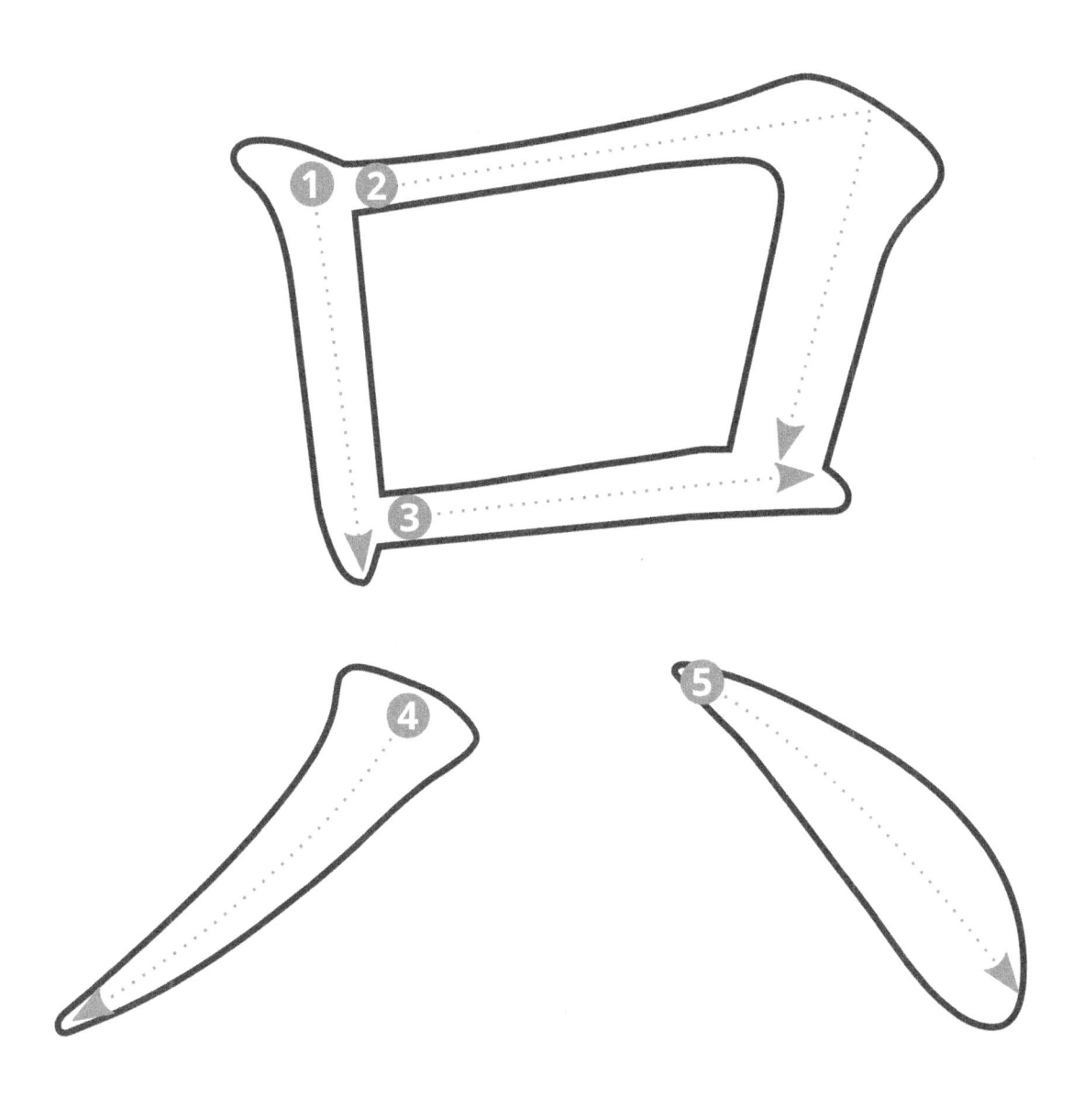

跟著「只」字從 ➡ 到 ★ 走出迷宮。
Follow the characters 只 from the arrow to the star to exit the maze.

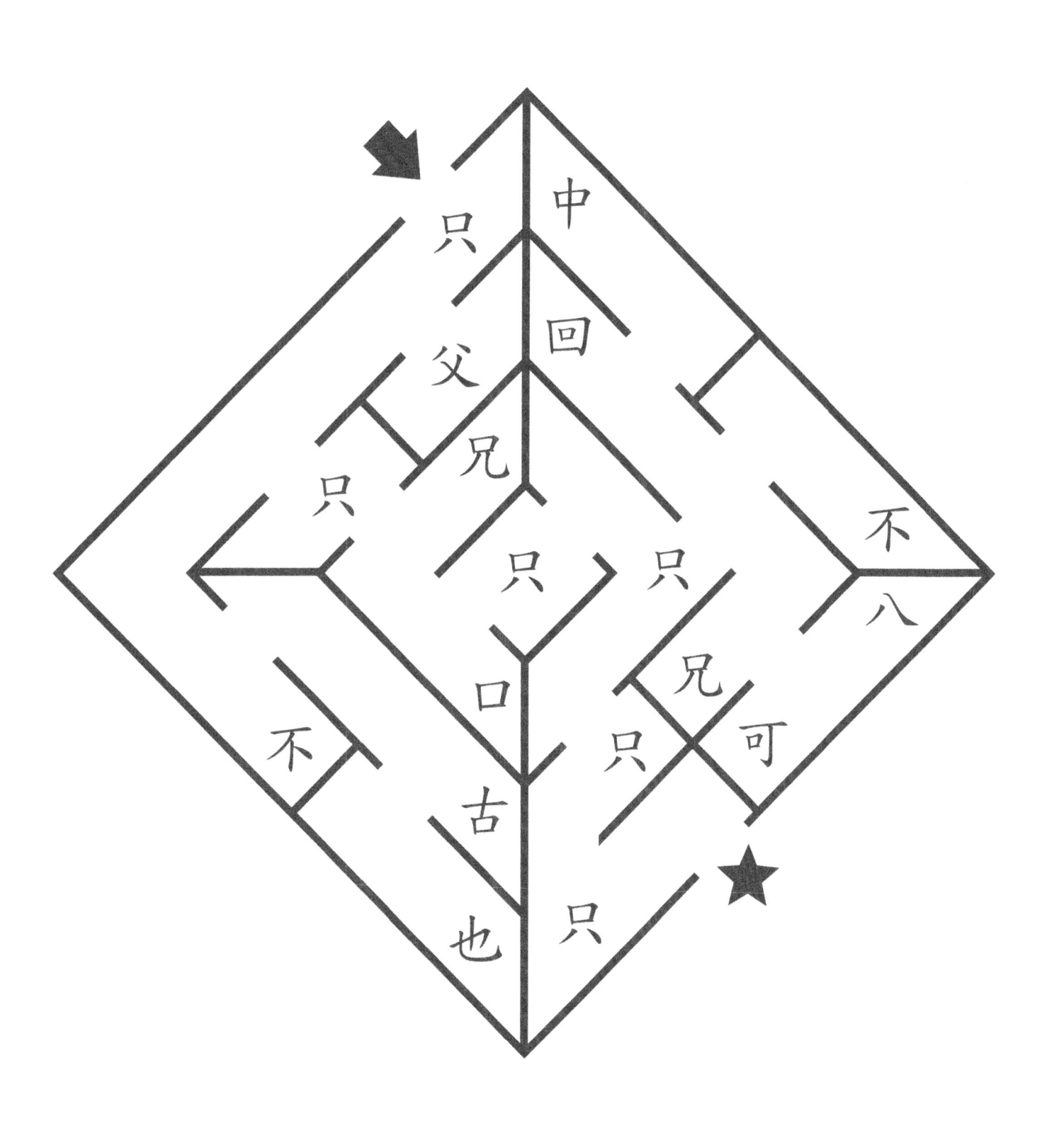

請將有「只」字的地方著色。
Color the areas with the character 只.

唸唸看
Read-Aloud

- 小鳥會在藍天上飛。
  Little birds can fly in the blue sky.

- 小貓只會在下頭走。
  The little cat can only walk beneath.

- 他明白他不會飛。
  He understands he cannot fly.

- 小貓不吃小鳥了。
  The little cat will not eat little birds.

- 他只想回到家中去了。
  He only wants to go back home.

恭喜你完成了這一課,請回到第一頁將本課的星星塗上顏色。
Congratulations! You have completed a lesson. Please color the star for this lesson on page 1.

82

第二十一課

Lesson 21 Sè – color

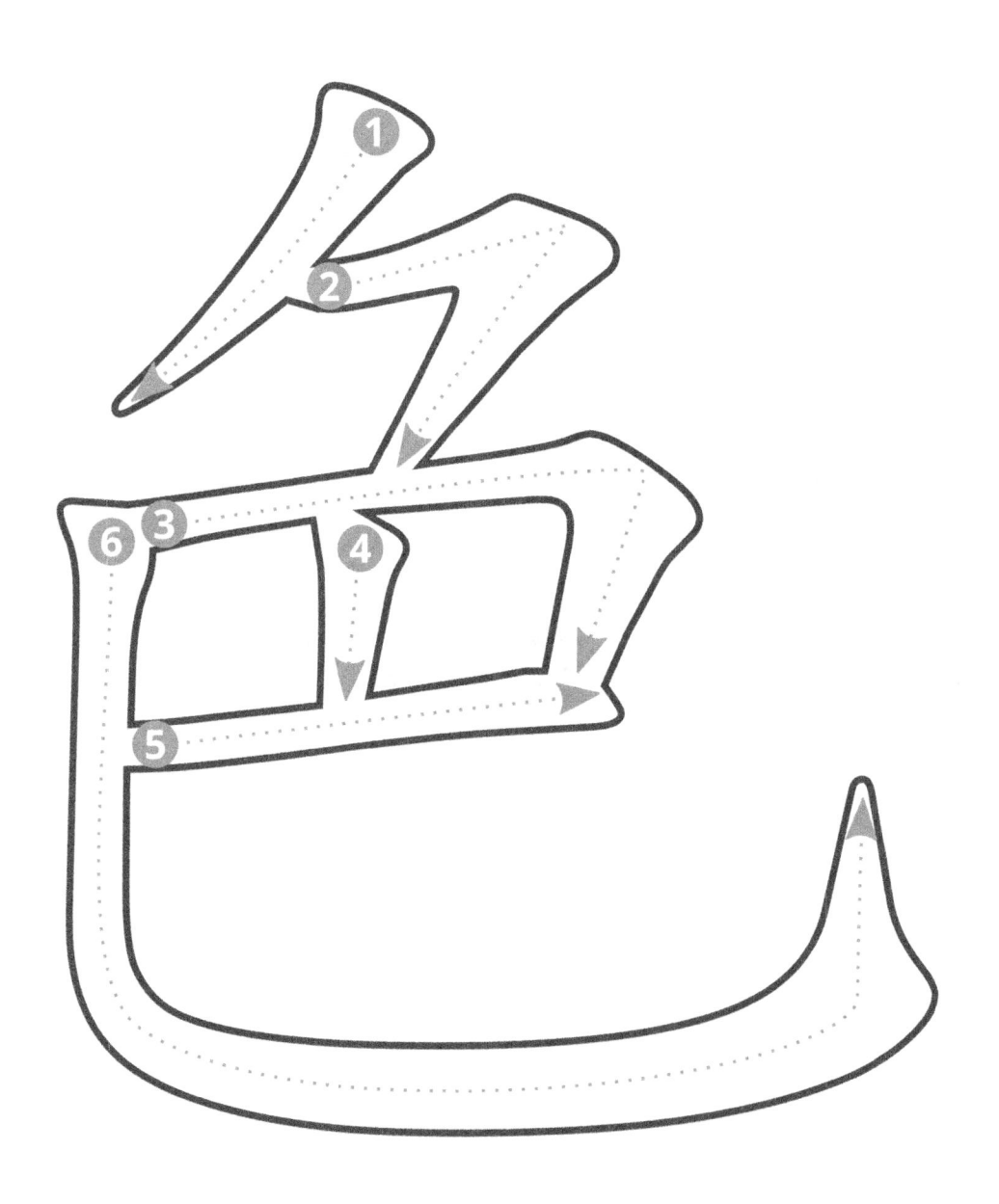

本書中的國字筆順是依據中華民國教育部「常用國字標準字體筆劃順序學習網」的筆劃順序彙編。
The stroke orders of the characters in this workbook follow the stroke orders provided on the "Learning Program for Stroke Order of Frequently Used Chinese Characters" website of the Ministry of Education, R.O.C. (Taiwan).

請找出三個能連成一線的顏色。
Please connect the same colors to win the tic-tac-toe.

紅色	藍色	紅色
白色	藍色	白色
紅色	藍色	白色

84

请將海灘球塗上裡面所寫的顏色。
Please color the beach ball with the indicated colors.

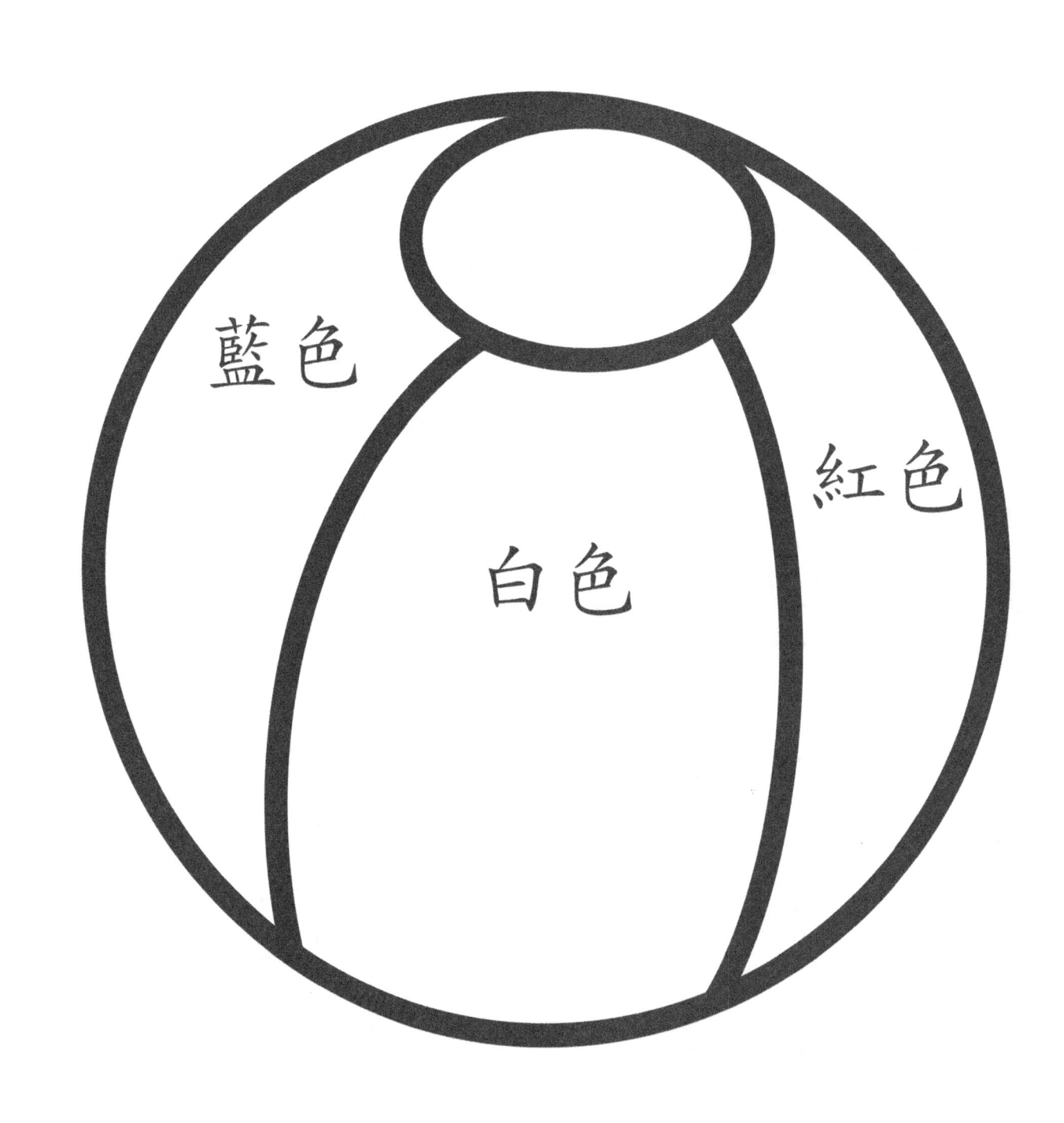

藍色
白色
紅色

唸唸看
Read-Aloud

- 他只愛藍色。
  He only loves the blue color.

- 可是地上沒有藍色的花。
  But there are no blue flowers on the ground.

- 他明白了。
  He understood.

- 只好要紅色的花了。
  (He) has no choice but to pick red flowers.

- 明天他會想要白色的。
  Tomorrow he will want white ones.

恭喜你完成了這一課,請回到第一頁將本課的星星塗上顏色。
Congratulations! You have completed a lesson. Please color the star for this lesson on page 1.

第二十二課

Lesson 22 Gěi – give

本書中的國字筆順是依據中華民國教育部「常用國字標準字體筆劃學習網」的筆劃順序彙編。
The stroke orders of the characters in this workbook follow the stroke orders provided on the "Learning Program for Stroke Order of Frequently Used Chinese Characters" website of the Ministry of Education, R.O.C. (Taiwan).

請將下方的字格剪下來讓孩子選擇正確的字貼上。
Please cut out the characters at the bottom and paste the correct ones.

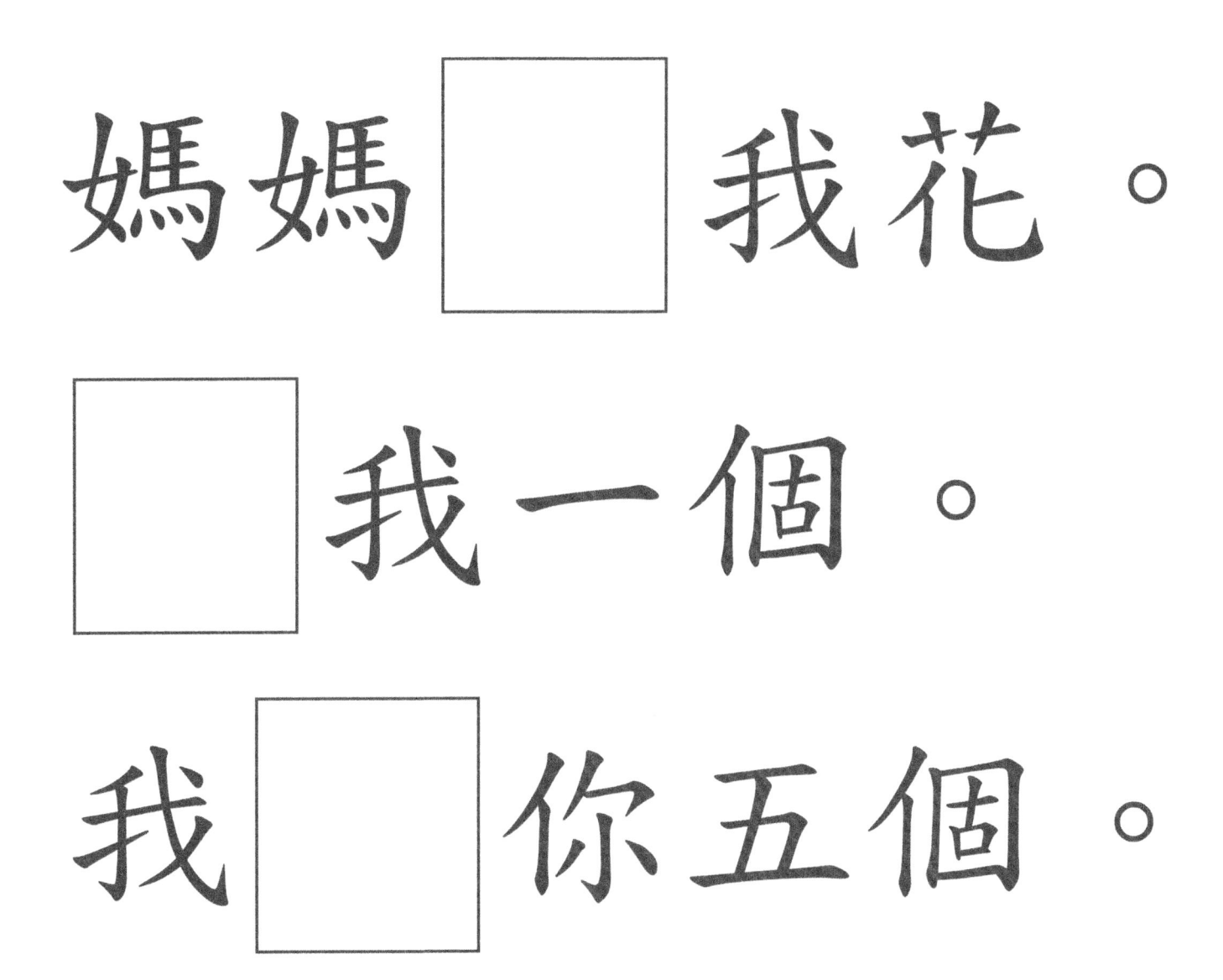

媽媽 ☐ 我花。

☐ 我一個。

我 ☐ 你五個。

| 合 | 給 | 給 | 給 | 合 |

找出到達「給」字的路。
Find the path leading to the character 給.

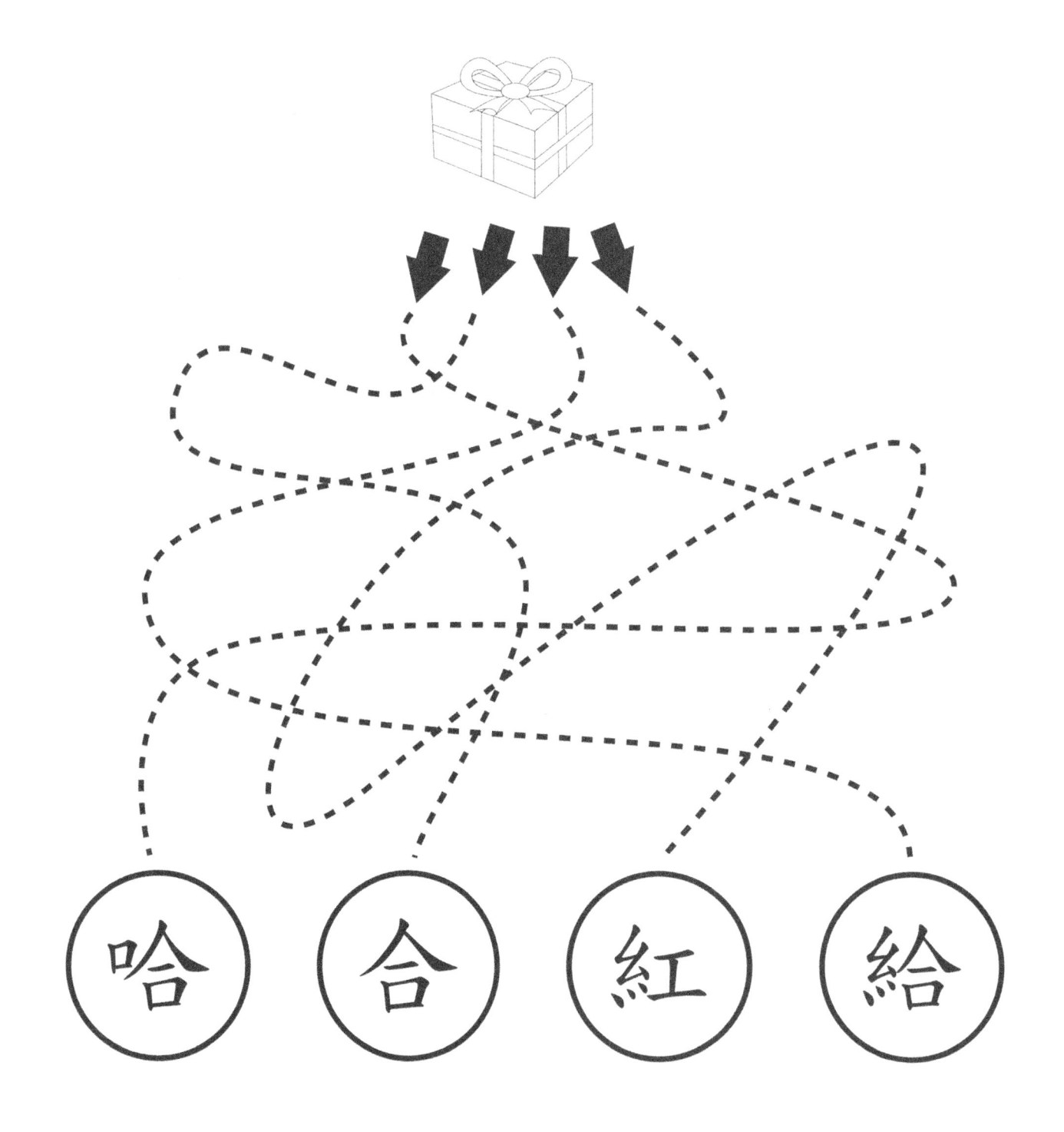

哈　合　紅　給

唸唸看
Read-Aloud

- 媽媽給他五隻藍色的鳥。
Mom gives him five blue birds.

- 他只愛藍色。
He only loves blue.

- 媽媽愛紅色。
Mom loves red.

- 他會給媽媽紅色的花。
He will give Mom red flowers.

- 明天他要上學。
Tomorrow he will go to school.

恭喜你完成了這一課,請回到第一頁將本課的星星塗上顏色。
Congratulations! You have completed a lesson. Please color the star for this lesson on page 1.

第二十三課

Lesson 23 Rì – day; sun

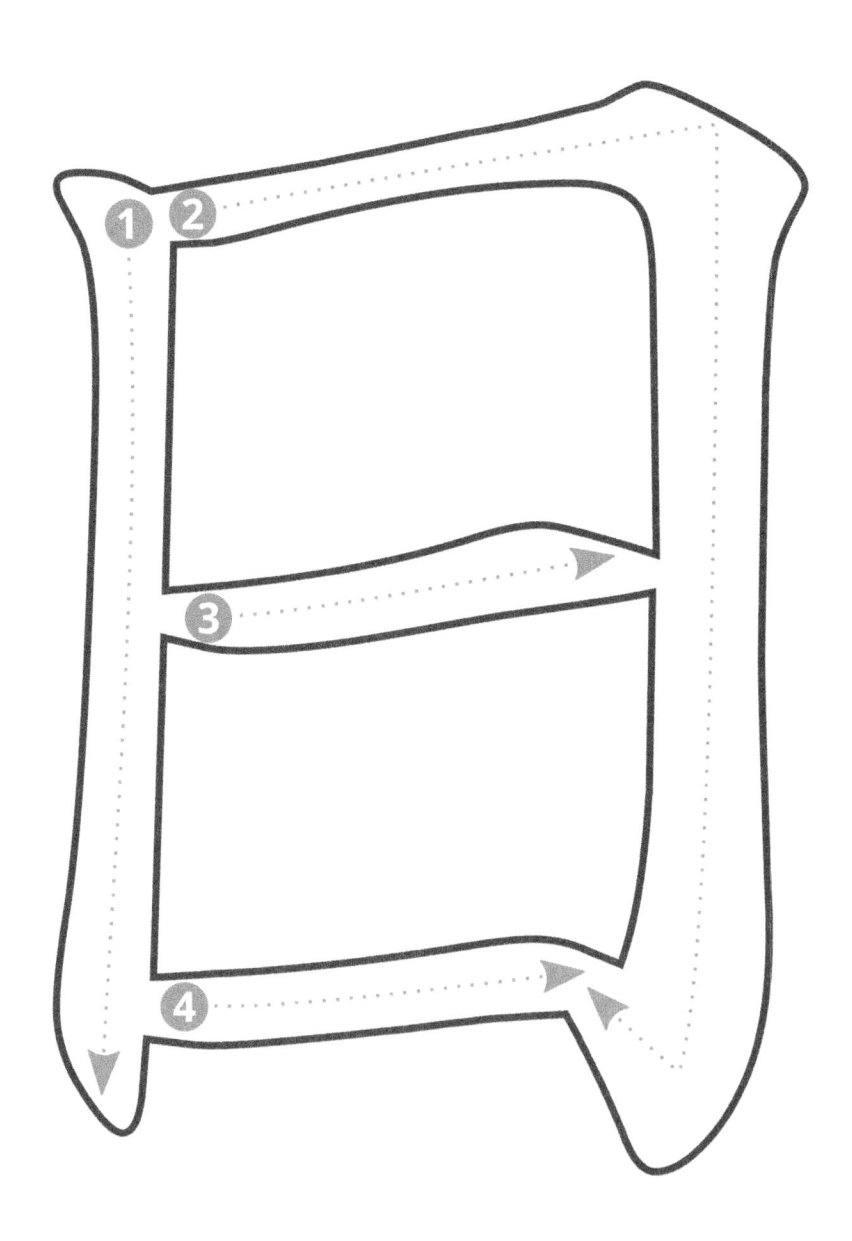

本書中的國字筆順是依據中華民國教育部「常用國字標準字體筆順學習網」的筆劃順序彙編。
The stroke orders of the characters in this workbook follow the stroke orders provided on the "Learning Program for Stroke Order of Frequently Used Chinese Characters" website of the Ministry of Education, R.O.C. (Taiwan).

「日」是象形字，中間的一橫是太陽而外框是光芒。
The character 日 is a pictograph, the middle line represents the sun and the outer frame represents the bright rays.

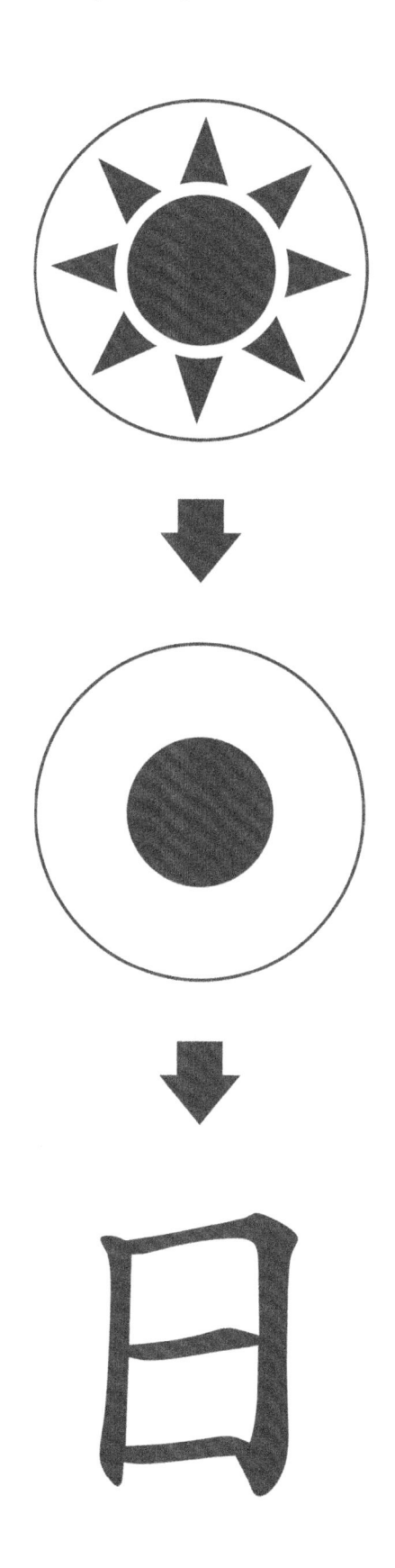

將有「日」字的太陽著色。
Color the suns with the character 日.

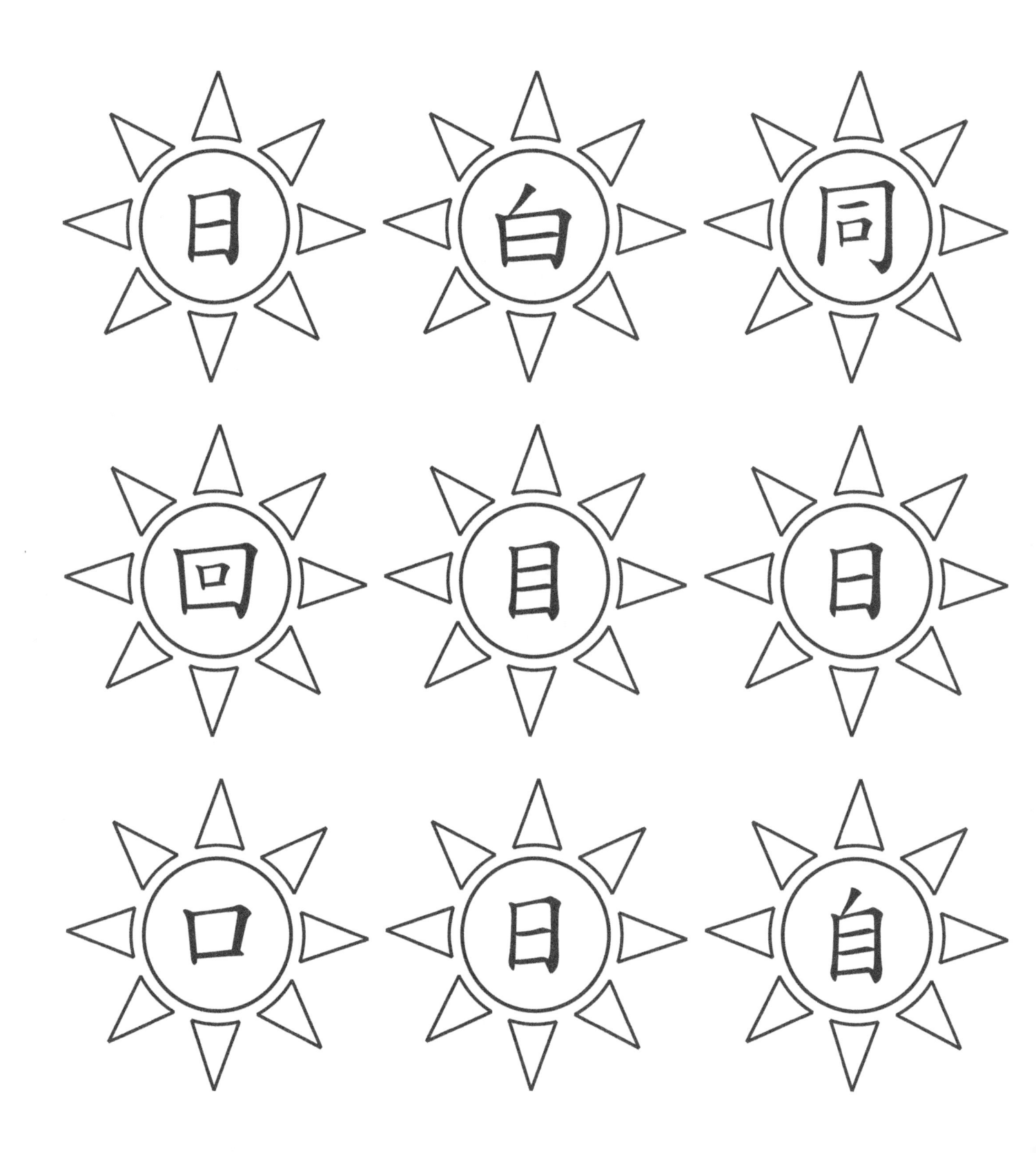

唸唸看
Read-Aloud

- 明天是爸爸的生日。
Tomorrow is Dad's birthday.

- 他會有一個生日會。
He will have a birthday party.

- 我會給他什麼？
What will I give him?

- 我會給他紅色的花。
I will give him red flowers.

- 我只想和爸爸在一起玩。
I only want to play with Dad.

恭喜你完成了這一課，請回到第一頁將本課的星星塗上顏色。
Congratulations! You have completed a lesson. Please color the star for this lesson on page 1.

第二十四課

Lesson 24 Zi – noun suffix
Zǐ – son; child

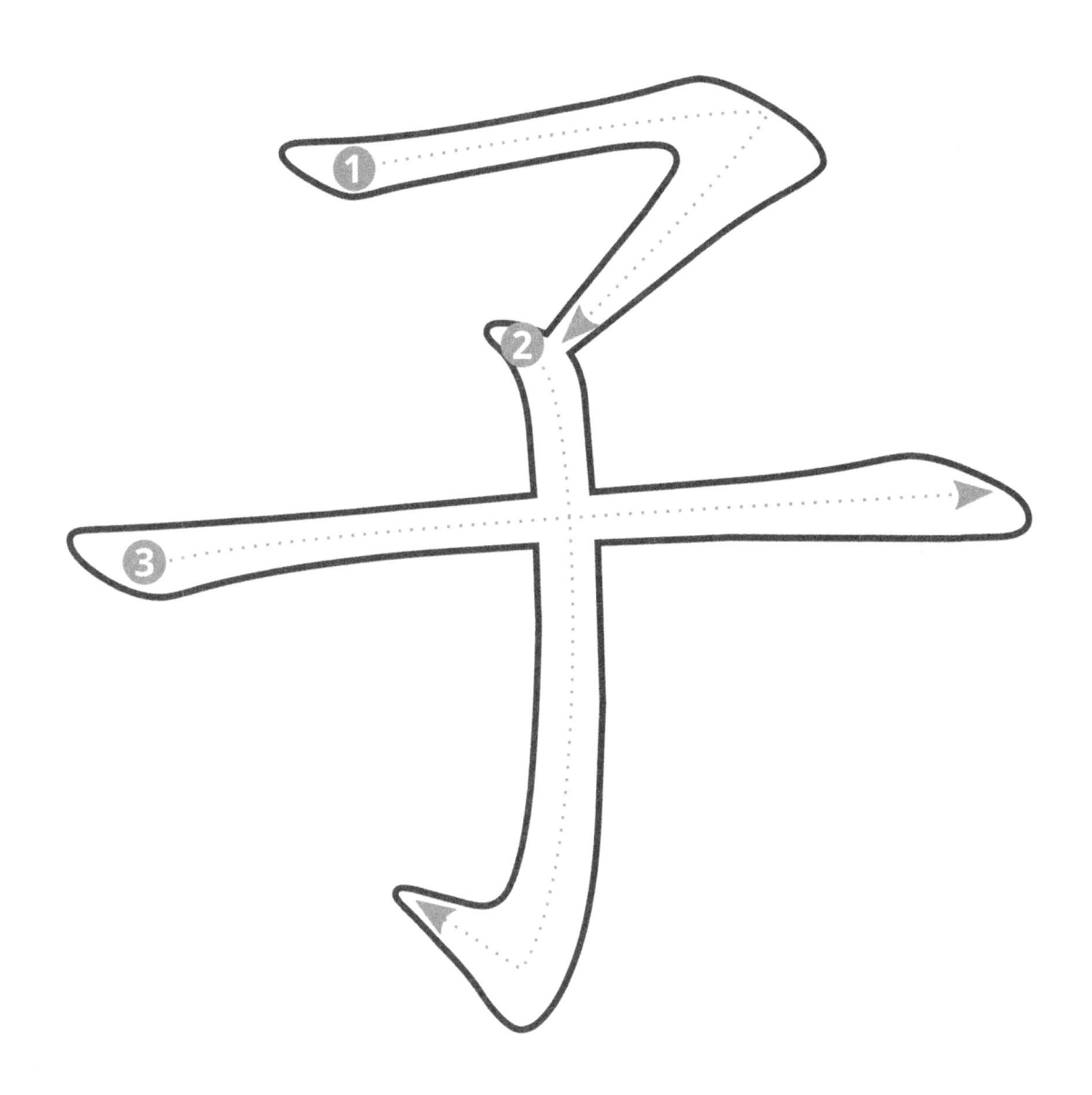

本書中的國字筆順是依據中華民國教育部「常用國字標準字體筆順學習網」的筆劃順序彙編。
The stroke orders of the characters in this workbook follow the stroke orders provided on the "Learning Program for Stroke Order of Frequently Used Chinese Characters" website of the Ministry of Education, R.O.C. (Taiwan).

「子」字是象形字，就像個孩子展開雙臂要媽媽抱的樣子。請將下圖著色。
The character 子 is a pictograph. It is a child with open arms wanting a hug from the mother. Please color the picture below.

將「子」字塗色幫助女孩找到回家的路。
Color the characters 子 to help the girl find the path home.

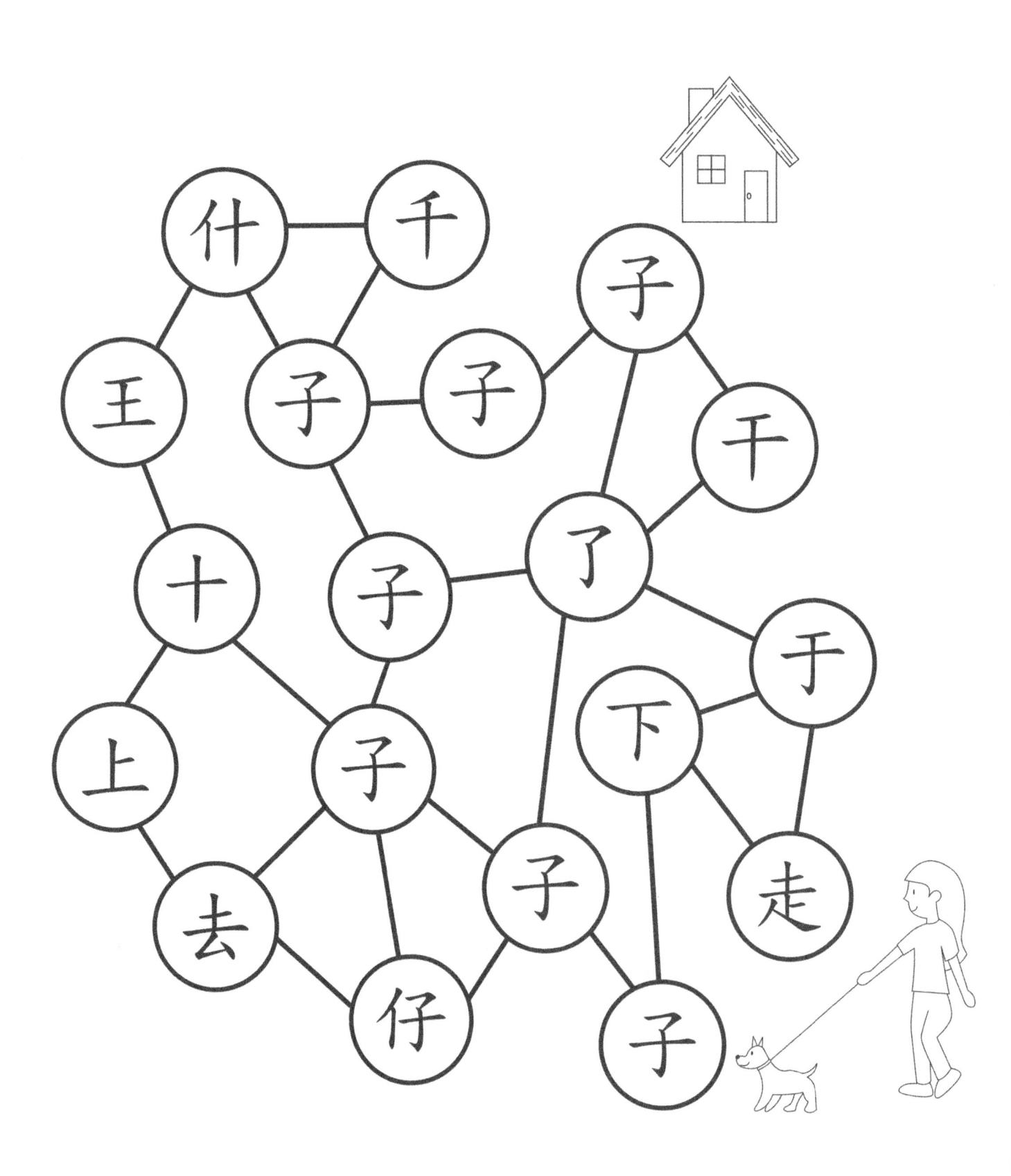

唸唸看
Read-Aloud

- 明天是一個好日子。
  Tomorrow is a good day.

- 明天也是小兔子的生日。
  Tomorrow is also the little rabbit's birthday.

- 爸爸會給他紅色的花吃。
  Dad will give him red flowers to eat.

- 小貓只會在家中。
  The little cat will only be at home.

- 小兔子會跳到爸爸的頭上去。
  The little rabbit will jump onto Dad's head.

恭喜你完成了這一課,請回到第一頁將本課的星星塗上顏色。
Congratulations! You have completed a lesson. Please color the star for this lesson on page 1.

第二十五課

Lesson 25 Kuài – fast; quick; soon

本書中的國字筆順是依據中華民國教育部「常用國字標準字體筆順學習網」的筆劃順序彙編。
The stroke orders of the characters in this workbook follow the stroke orders provided on the "Learning Program for Stroke Order of Frequently Used Chinese Characters" website of the Ministry of Education, R.O.C. (Taiwan).

將「快」字連到速度快的東西。
Connect the character 快 to things that are fast.

快

跟著「快」字從 ➡ 到 ★ 走出迷宮。
Follow the characters 快 from the arrow to the star to exit the maze.

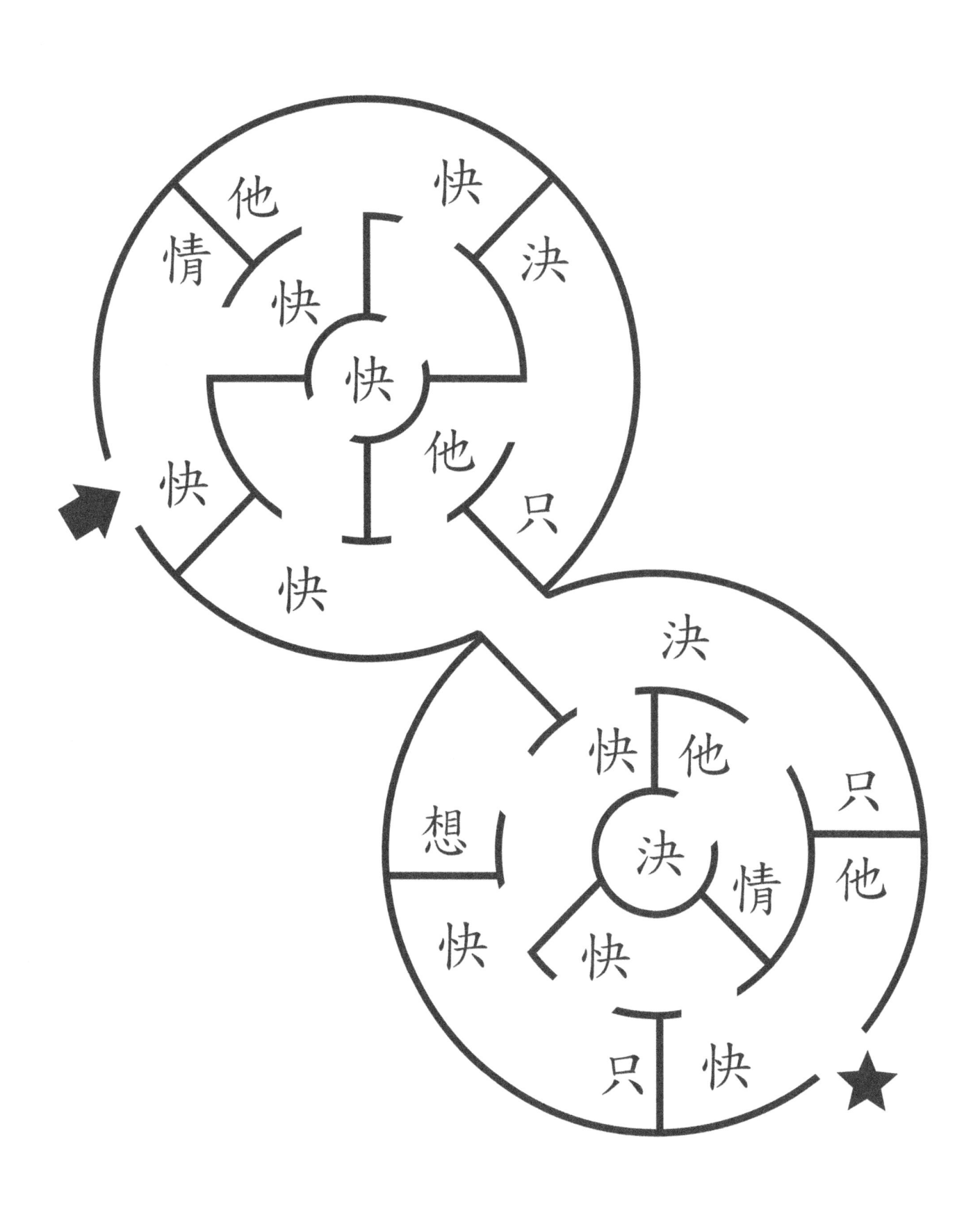

唸唸看
Read-Aloud

- 白色的兔子好快。
  The white rabbit is so fast.

- 只是他不會飛。
  But he cannot fly.

- 他生日快要到了。
  His birthday is coming soon.

- 他想要我給他好吃的。
  He wants me to give him something good to eat.

- 他只愛紅色的花。
  He only loves red flowers.

恭喜你完成了這一課,請回到第一頁將本課的星星塗上顏色。
Congratulations! You have completed a lesson. Please color the star for this lesson on page 1.

獎 狀
Certificate of Achievement

恭喜

Congratulations to

_____

完成趣味識字第三冊。
特發此狀以資鼓勵！

for completing Fun with Chinese Workbook 3.

_____ _____

簽名 Signature　　　　　　　　　　　日期 Date